America, Judgement of the Republic for which it Stands

"One Nation Under God"

By

© Steven B Riddley

Scriptor House LLC

2810 N Church St Wilmington, Delaware, 19802

www.scriptorhouse.com

Phone: +1302-205-2043

Published by Scriptor House LLC

Paperback ISBN: 979-8-88692-103-8

eBook ISBN: 979-8-88692-104-5

From the Author's desk

These are chronicles written after the book of Revelation was revealed to me in a simple way for all to understand this book of mysteries, consisting of General Information messages reflecting observations of our time in the downfall of America through he eyes of the prophets. This second of the two-book set of the Obama and Trump Presidency as in the numbers 44 & 45 represent and interesting parallel in biblical history. These two presidents will fuel all the hidden evils to the point of seeing violence on a scale we have never seen before in this nation. Their influence will carry-over in the people affected during their term. After they have served their purpose in this office as kings of the free world, number 44 will legalize homosexuality, the sin that cannot be reversed and therefore, bring the delayed judgement without remedy.

Number 45 will judge the church as a lying spirit that will show the evangelical confessing Christians their state of delusion as a lying spirit that will say the right things at the wrong time in history to get their attention. The state of this nation's governmental corruption will be what will cause many to follow his narcissistic behavior in this high office as president of the free world. We as a nation will be under a strong blinding delusion that will expose the divisions in this nation as the confessing Christian Church, local and state governments, and the three branches of government in Washington will become so divided, it will send us into an economic depression that will cause our enemies to reap the spoils of a collapse nation that was the envy of the world. The detail of our downfall is written in my book on Revelation under the title; **"BIBLICAL PROPHETIC CHRONICLES OF THE LAST GENERATION."**

Contents

Times, Ages and Dispensations

Regardless of what doctrine you practice, the only doctrine that will endure the test of this last generation is that the apostles brought on the day of Pentecost. The tribulation period will be second stage of Earth's time continuum of restoration through apocalyptic changes that the natural man would not survive if not removed.

First, the restoration of the one church established in Christ; **second,** the gathering of the elect of Israel and the church; **third**, the renovation and restoration of the geography of the earth set back to the time of Adam that will take seven years to complete. The first sign will begin will be "9/11/01". God will begin to reveal the evils of mankind and his present state from the church to the government as well as all the evils of this society as a nation. This will account for the beginning stages of the natural disaster signs in that last generation of gentiles in a nation that was responsible for the restoration and protection of Israel, America. The forthcoming writings are to educate you on what we all fail to learn from the whole council of the teaching of the Holy Spirit. This is the relationship God desired of all his children as found in … **Jeremiah 33:3 (KJV) ³ Call unto me, and I will answer thee, and shew thee great and mighty things, which thou knowest not. Ephesians 3:5 (KJV) ⁵ Which in other ages was not made known unto the sons of men, as it is now revealed unto his holy apostles and prophets by the Spirit; This is what Jesus will reveal to his children whose minds have been transformed to receive it.**

These are my Enoch moments with Christ

There are many unexplained mysteries in the bible that are in single verse form. This is the door open to those that are invited into the throne room of knowledge to hear things that are beyond man's comprehension. Everything God said can be found locked in His word; the bible.

Now let's look at some of these passages that contain hidden mysteries.

Genesis 1:1-2 (KJV) 1 In the beginning God created the heaven and the earth. (This is Earth's origin) 2 And the earth was without form, and void; (This is what it looked like. The void is a giant mass of water covering it in the heavens above it. and darkness was upon the face of the deep. It was not seen as a live planet until he gave it life. And the Spirit of God moved upon the face of the waters. Now here's the mystery of where the water come from?**) Genesis 1:7 (KJV) 6 and God said, let there be a firmament in the midst of the waters, and let it divide the waters from the waters.** (Now to understand what was happening naturally, the firmament is the sky which was a void of water that was transferred from the sky to the Earth as water to enter the ground; by taking the water from the sky and putting it into the ground as in)… **7 And God made the firmament, and divided the waters which were under the firmament from the waters which were above the firmament: and it was so. Genesis 1:9 (KJV) 9 And God said, Let the waters under the heaven be gathered together unto one place,** ((Now what was this one place?) **and let the dry land appear: and it was so.** All the water from the firmament went into the deep of the earth that was to supply life to the subsequent life that was going to be created that would need it to live.

When all this was completed, all that was left was dry land over the face of the earth. After creation, where did the water come from if not from the sky? **Genesis 2:6 "(KJV) 6 But there went up a mist from the earth and watered the whole face of the ground."** (Now you see the whole face of the earth was just land. There was no mention of mountains or oceans. The next is our origin as a human being created in the image of his creator, God.**) Genesis 1:26-28 "(KJV) 26 And God said, let us make man in our image, after our likeness: and let them have dominion over the fish of the sea, and over the fowl of the air, and over the cattle, and over all the earth, and over every creeping thing that crept upon the earth. 27 So God created man in his own image, in the image of God created he him; male and female created he them. 28 And God blessed them, and God said unto them, be fruitful, and multiply, and replenish the earth, and subdue it: and have dominion over the fish of the sea, and over the fowl of the air, and over every living thing that moveth upon the earth."**

This is who Adam is before the fall and what he was given the authority to rule over; everything in the natural that God created. The whole earth was inhabited by creatures of God's creation. To account for the origin of species, each had to be given a name. Adam with the mind of God gave a name to all the species of God's creation that was to cover the face of the earth before the flood. Through his free-will, unknown to him at the time, his female counter part will yield to act on the word of a condemned high ark dethroned angel name Lucifer, she will be used to test his obedience to only hear the voice of his creator. The curious nature of his counterpart and comforter Eve, will be use to speak to him once he (Satan) has condemned her, having acted on his enticing words of a condemned angel convert her state mind to become a natural human in the image of her creator. Satan will speak through her now to get Adam to lose his place as having the authority over all the Earth. When he yielded to act on Eve's word to bite the forbidden fruit, Satan at that time took possession of the Earth. Therefore, defiling all creation and causing them to turn against each other as now becoming mediums to procreate evil spirits.

The revelation of the New Testament man after the resurrection of Christ, he now is the new Adam with the same authority as the first Adam. He (man) is to become the truly born-again from above as Christ, the second Adam to restore what the first Adam lost and give it back to you. I just had to take a break after this and meditate on it for a while to sink in. Now let's get to the animals. Man, in his fallen state down through dispensations has found large fossils unearthed by archeologist who without this mystery will compare this to man and his stature without knowing, through his own willing ignorance would assume they are before the creation.

Now if man could live to reach the age of 969 years as the bible record is the age of Methuselah at his death; what about some of these animal species that grow to become very large to the point that were on various land masses on the face of the earth at that time. All the animal species fed on the vegetations before the flood. When Adam sinned, all things begin to turn on each other as Cain did to Able. The spirits of evil were released upon the earth to possess all the species of God's creation that originated from his breath of life. Large beast begins to turn on each other as in a fight for territory and in this process, begin to devourer one-another.

The evidence that debunks the scientific view of man's origin and the so called pre-historic age is found in the bellies of some of these large animal fossils that had partially or undigested food while in a preserved state of their untimely death. This is one of the grey arears that lends itself to the birth of science by trying to make sense of the unexplained phenomenon of his pursuits in mans quest for knowledge. God directed the animals that were to be taken through the flood to march to the Ark by twos. The larger species we know as scientist call pre-historic had grown too large because of the 100% oxygen level in the earth and he knew they would not be able to live in the crossover, therefore, caused them to perish in the flood. They are the fossils found by archeologist that were carried all over the world today.

The flood carried the evidence of their remains that will be found in places all over the world that archeologist in later dispensations of time will unearth. Even with this new modern technology, man has yet to discover how these civilizations built these phenomenal structures with such precision. Look at the rims of the Grand Canyon walls and the rocks in monument valley in Arizona; can you say they are not caused by receding water marks of another time in the created history of the earth? Now whose report are you ready to receive, man's or God's? Now man's thoughts are what his father the devil tells him to believe. Take for example, the cosmos; the mystery is so far from man as its's origin, all he can do is theorize according to his imagination.

Another scripture that's shrouded in a mystery

John 10:16 "(KJV) 16 And other sheep I have, which are not of this fold: them also I must bring, and they shall hear my voice; and there shall be one-fold, and one shepherd." Now let's go back to the beginning to get the answer to this mystery. When Adam sinned, through him Satan defiled everything God created at that moment when he yielded to act on Eve's suggestion to partake of her sin. The two united together against what God told them not to do. Satan was already judged, hell was prepared for him and his angels; therefore, now under his curse as his child, our punishment is as his if we don't repent. After they partook of the sin of disobedience together, Satan can now pro-create his own children through them. According to … **1 John 3:12 "(KJV) 12 Not as Cain, who was of that wicked one, and slew his brother. And wherefore slew he him? Because his own works were evil, and his brothers righteous. John 8:44 (KJV) 44 Ye are of your father the devil, and the lusts of your father ye will do. He was a murderer from the beginning, and abode not in the truth, because there is no truth in him. When he speaketh a lie, he speaketh of his own: for he is a liar, and the father of it."** This was the first evidenced at the beginning. Every one of us will be born with these characteristics of his evil DNA that has now defiled us all. The only good God now recognized in the earth is himself in the seeds God chooses for his own. This is what he told Adam after they sinned … **Genesis 6:1 "(KJV) 1 And it came to pass, when men began to multiply on the face of the earth, and daughters were born unto them,"** Remember, in the beginning the earth was one giant land mass to be inhabited by man and beast breathing 100% oxygen to regenerate their cells that caused him to live hundreds of years. **Genesis 6:4 "(KJV) 4 There were giants in the earth in those days; and also, after that, when the sons of God** (*Watcher angels*) **came in unto the daughters of men, and they bare children to them, the same became mighty men which were of old, men of renown."** This act not only cause the increase of evil but the mixing of angelic DNA with natural mankind caused their off springs to grow as tall as archeologist have found to be as least eighteen feet in height. In those days after Adam was driven out of the Garden of Eden, all these things begin to multiply exponentially all over the earth in great numbers. When Cain was cast out from among his family, I am not at liberty to disclose things that are not relevant to man's current state as God have him to be. These watcher angels were to record the deeds of men while being in the Antediluvian time when man was being judged by his conscious with-out the law as God winked on man's ignorance to gather souls in the book of life of a hidden time before the flood that Enoch's writings became history. God could not let this knowledge in the presence of the devil, be revealed in the crossover to a new time continuum after the flood.

God was gathering sheep of another fold in that dispensation that he chose not to reveal these mysteries recorded by Enoch as written after the flood. Therefore, Noah only brought through a small portion of Enoch's records that became pertinent to the genesis of what contributed to the fall of God's creation. The first and last dispensations of time of the natural earth for mankind will be the gathering of the greatest number of saints to live for eternity.

There are many worlds in God's universal cosmos he created; that mystery will be seen by those He choose to spend eternity with Him. **Revelation 7:9 "(KJV) 9 After this I beheld, and, lo, a great multitude, which no man could number, of all nations, and kindreds, and people, and tongues, stood before the throne, and before the Lamb, clothed with white robes, and palms in their hands;"** Another mystery, all things God created in in heaven has His spirit, therefore, what form it appears in is irrelevant to Him because we all are as one. Now this is what happened after the flood; **Genesis 9:1 "(KJV) 1 And God blessed Noah and his sons, and said unto them, be fruitful, and multiply, and replenish the earth".**

After the flood, only 1/3 of the land mass was left for mankind to replenish. Who knows how many God has chosen during these times. There are about seven billion people in the world now to occupy this small amount of land left after the flood. A man by the name of Ken Hovine gave this revelation at the time when the school system was introducing Darwinism to be taught in public school and they suppressed his evidence and brought him up on charges to put him in prison. This was the work of the members of the secret society to keep the people dumb down to be taken over in the last generation by Satan that will come literally riding over the airwaves as in … **Ephesians 2:2 "(KJV) 2 Wherein in time past ye walked according to the course of this world, (In man) according to the <u>prince of the power of the air</u>, the spirit that now worketh in the children of disobedience:"** (This is the generation of the children he would claim by taking over their minds through a new technologies that will take control of man through the airwaves we know as the internet and the smart phone. Just as history is always repeating itself in the bible as in these two examples. The former and the latter rain, the Alpha of the world and the Omega of the world. What happen in the Alpha of the world will be repeated at the end which is the Omega of the world.

Under grace and truth per the resurrection of Christ, Pentecost brought the return of Adam, the Alpha man in the former rain. After two thousand years, Satan seduce the church that cause the loss of the gospel, Christ will bring back Adam as the Omega man in the latter rain; therefore, the closing of another time continuum.

The tribulation period of seven years in our time represents Noah's seven days before the rain. This is when God will restore through tribulation not only the presents of Christ church as the one God but the natural disasters, we are now experiencing are part of the changing geography of the Earth. Taking us back the Alpha of time so man can once again live for hundreds of years as the enemy of his soul is bound in … **Revelation 20:3 "(KJV) 3 And cast him into the bottomless pit, and shut him up, and set a seal upon him, that he should deceive the nations no more, till the thousand years should be fulfilled: and after that he must be loosed a little season."** The Earth will be purified by fire in the tribulation and the final purification will take place at the end of the last millennium. The last millennium will be the age of perfect law the before the third and final trauma of the Earth takes place when Satan is loosed again after this final prophecy is fulfilled … **Isaiah 45:23 "(KJV) 23 I have sworn by myself, the word is gone out of my mouth in righteousness, and shall not return, that unto me every knee shall bow, every tongue shall swear."** A remnant of every tribe, kindred and tongue was selected to survive the tribulation to fulfill this prophecy to literally come to the city of Jerusalem to worship at the throne of Jesus. These are they that were protected during the tribulation to repopulate the earth for the last time. **Isaiah 26:20 "(KJV) 20 Come, my people, enter thou into thy chambers, and shut thy doors about thee: hide thyself as it were for a little moment, until the indignation be over past."** This passage of scripture tells us how God is divinely protecting a remnant to repopulate the earth.

The reason why Satan is released at the end, many of those seeds were cursed never to enter the kingdom but because their father Satan is bound during the millennium, they could not be tempted. They were Satan's children's and therefore could not manifest the evils of their father while he was bound. When he is loosed, at the end of the last millennium, he will claim them in his last act of rebellion and they along with him will be cast into the lake of fire at the great white throne judgment. **Revelation 20:10 "(KJV) 10 And the devil that deceived them was cast into the lake of fire and brimstone, where the beast and the false prophet are, and shall be tormented day and night for ever and ever. Revelation 20:14-15 (KJV) 14 And death and hell were cast into the lake of fire. This is the second death. 15 And whosoever was not found written in the book of life was cast into the lake of fire."**

The book of life

Revelation 13:8 "(KJV) 8 And all that dwell upon the earth shall worship him, *(These are the children given over to the devil)* **whose names are not written in the book of life of the Lamb slain from the foundation of the world. Revelation 20:12 (KJV) 12 And I saw the dead, small and great, stand before God; and the books were opened** *(There were more than two books that was open at the final judgment. This mystery will be revealed for all to see at that time.)* **and another books were opened, which is the book of life: and the dead were judged out of those things which were written in the books, according to their works."**

This is one of the great mysteries about the above scriptures. In the beginning, the watcher angels were there to record the deeds in the life of everyone born in the image of God. That is the book of life that came from God that all will have to give an account of.

That's from Adam to Jesus which included the law because the law did not make man sinless in the flesh; that's why all who died under the law went to Paradise at death. **Revelation 21:27 "(KJV) 27 and there shall in no wise enter into it any thing that defileth, neither whatsoever worketh abomination, or maketh a lie: but they which are written in the Lamb's book of life."** Now under grace and truth, we have the lamb's book of life. The souls in the book of life that died with sin in their life but are given mercy at death as according to the manner of law at that time under the old covenant. This is Satan role as the accuser of the brethren, was cast out of heaven because of sin found in him; therefore, no sin can enter heaven. He had the right to bound the people under the law for their sins. This is why Paradise was created to retain them until the lamp, slain before the foundation paid the price to release them.

This is the justification that gave him the keys to Paradise, death and hell. This statement may shock you, If you are given over to him for his use, he has the power to send you to hell as his children at his own will if your name is not written in the book of life. This brings us to the two judgments that take place in heaven. The first is the … **Revelation 20:11 "(KJV) 11 And I saw a great**

white throne, and him that sat on it, from whose face the earth and the heaven fled away; and there was found no place for them". This is the last judgment at the end. Those in the lamb's book of life are judged after the rapture.

This includes all born from Adam to the second resurrection of those in Christ church. He paid the sin price to release these souls gathered up until that time to be released and transferred to the third heaven. Now, all that will enter heaven thereafter will have to come through Christ by way of the **lamb's book of life**.

These are chosen from the foundation of the world, elected by the father to become his bride to show the glory of the father to the world through these chosen ones. They will do the exploits during the tribulation that will be the return of spirit of Moses and Elijah to show the world who is the one true God. They will become his bride that will come up in the second resurrection in … **Revelation 14:15-20 "(KJV) ¹⁵ And another angel came out of the temple, crying with a loud voice to him that sat on the cloud, thrust in thy sickle, and reap: for the time is come for thee to reap; for the harvest of the earth is ripe. ¹⁶ And he that sat on the cloud thrust in his sickle on the earth; and the earth was reaped.** (This is when the rapture will take place) **¹⁷ And another angel came out of the temple which is in heaven, he also having a sharp sickle. ¹⁸ And another angel came out from the altar, which had power over fire; and cried with a loud cry to him that had the sharp sickle, saying, Thrust in thy sharp sickle, and gather the clusters of the vine of the earth; for her grapes are fully ripe."** (These are the children of disobedience turned over to the devil for the destruction of their flesh as the unwise virgins; they were God's children prayed for by the prayers of the saints that gave their lives for them. This will be the reaping of the harvest during the second half of the tribulation period to become the bride of Christ at the marriage supper of the lamb.

Now there's the Great white throne judgment; all whose names are not written in the lamb's book of life are being judged at the end of the last millennium. These were children being judged from Adam to that time of the end of the last millennium who had their names blotted out of the lamb's book of like by having sins of omission. They were the soles given over to the devil for his use after the fall of Adam throughout times, ages, and dispensations. **(Gal. 5:19-21)** The devil justified claiming them. They were weight in the balance and found wanting. **(Dan. 5:27)** Now the children of the Satan will   receive the reward of their father the devil. **Revelation 20:14-15 "(KJV) ¹⁴ And death and hell were cast into the lake of fire. This is the second death. ¹⁵ And** whosoever was not found written in the book of life was cast into the lake of fire. Revelation 16:13 (KJV)[13] And I saw three unclean spirits like frogs come out of the mouth of the dragon, and out of the mouth of the beast, and out of the mouth of the false prophet. Revelation 19:20 (KJV) [20] And the beast was taken, and with him the false prophet that wrought miracles before him, with which he deceived them that had received the mark of the beast, and them that worshipped his image. These both were cast alive into a lake of fire burning with brimstone. Revelation 20:10 (KJV) [10] And the devil that deceived them was cast into the lake of fire and brimstone, where the beast and the false prophet are, and shall be tormented day and night for ever and ever." This is knowledge that comes with the revelation of Jesus Christ that is among the few there be that find him. God is the judge of all mankind he created; therefore, many will be given mercy by making their calling sure when they receive these words through his elects.

First impressions of the gospel are not always the right ones

"The mystery of self-deliverance"

* * * * * * * * * * * * * * * * * * * *

It is my prayer and hope that the few that receive these chronicles are reading, studying and meditating on them. As I have mentioned in the previous chronicles. I was a confessing Christian for twenty years before I had what was a real corrective encounter with the truth. All that time, I was operating in the permissive will of God. I followed the influences of mans doctrine as in a denominational setting for eleven years. This was in May of 1972 when I joined the church in a Disciples of Christ Denomination. I, as a child grew up under this teaching in name only as I would find out later. I was serious about pastors telling truth. When I attended convocational meetings, after the sessions were over, many smoked cigarettes as they huddled together joking and jesting about worldly things. I knew some of these men as a child. I grew up around a religious environment as a child. I now realize I am an answer to my grandmother's prayers. Little did I know for this to come to pass, I would embark upon a journey that would take thirty years to completely come to the knowledge of the truth?

I was a church hopper at the time as pastors would call you. I was looking for a man who practiced what he preached. This was my encounters with denominations and pastors. I went from my childhood denomination as Disciples of Christ to the Pentecostal Holiness Movement. Although I visited some Baptist churches, some of their pastors even had girlfriends on the side. All this happen in the first eleven years of my search for truth. You see, I was looking for it through man at the time. My lack of spiritual satisfaction and contentment would end up in a domestic confusion that led to a near tragedy by having been labeled as a church hopper. In my zealous search, I neglected my family because of my tendency to be one tract minded in my pursuits. During this time, I thought I was right because I could see others faults and not my own. I saw what others didn't notice with-out knowing I was judging them. I was a modern-day Pharisee.

God had always had his hand upon me but like Paul, I was too zealous and blind to see him at the time. After being separated from my first wife, I traveled with an evangelist a crossed the country until I reached Phoenix Arizona. The evangelist group I traveled with disbanded, and I was literally left behind. I didn't need to watch a movie to know what that's like. Although I tried to reconcile with my ex-wife, I was divorce by having irreconcilable differences. When I found myself alone in a strange city, no one to call or communicate with because I had been ridiculed for separating from my family to prevent a major tragedy that would have resulted in the loss of my life through domestic circumstances caused by my blind religious zeal. I am being transparent to you all that read this because I became a victim of my blind religious zeal. I knew I had a calling on my life. I know why so many bad experiences had to happen to me to get my attention. I found out that the devil knows who has a spiritual mark on them that prevents him from destroying you when God has a purpose for your life.

All I ever wanted to do was be a good servant as a confessing Christian but sought it through the eyes of men that cause me to move ahead of God. Only God could have rescued me to find my answer to the peace and rest spiritually I needed. Now that I was all alone, God open a spiritual door while in that broken state of mind in a motel room in a bad section of town; there alone, I met Satan in the spirit. This was orquistrated by God for my benefit so later I would know the depth of the enemy of our soul has on us from with-in.

One evening while lying in a fetal position in bed, so depressed to where I felt knots in my stomach that took my apatite. This evil spirit came into the room so strong that I felt I was dying; I instinctively knew it was Satan. He began telling me what people was saying about me in my hometown and how God had no more use for me, he tried to get me to commit suicide. I had no strength to resist his evil powers and just when I thought I would die, he would leave.

Not knowing when he would return to torment me, during a course of three weeks, he visited me three times. I would always lie in a fetal position to hold on to my sanity. I tried to take my life after his taunting visits but couldn't get the nerve to follow through. He convinced me that God no longer had any use for me. Beloved, I don't want any one to have this type of encounter for God to get your attention, but only God knows what he is doing to get the results needed to become a soldier of his cross.

I know I'm not alone in this experience, this is to give some of you hope that have not made wise decisions in your life that cause you to suffer the loss of all things and family at the hand of your own ignorance. Satan is real and if you ever meet him like this with-out God in it, you are going to die. I found out how the spirit of suicide is activated if your number is up? That's when Satan sends the sickle angels from hell to take you there.

My first impression of the false doctrine nearly got me literally killed. I was a chosen vessel to the point that I didn't get to live the easy comfortable life that many are deceived into thinking is the way of Christ. He used these experiences to show me who he really is beyond a shadow of doubt. My zeal to tell it like it is with no understanding of what kind of reaction I would receive as a young minister during that time, not being born from above but as a zealous person under man's teaching. **"I had a zeal for God but not according to knowledge". (Rom. 10:2)** My impact provoked the whole Christian community in my hometown at that time. I did not know then what I come to know later that the hand of God was working all things out to my good to give me an experience that would seal the depth of my present convictions in faith to speak truth that cause me to suffer the many rejections along the way. **2 Timothy 3:12 "(KJV) [12] Yea, and all that will live godly in Christ Jesus shall suffer persecution."** I was not that godly at the time and suffered for my ignorance. I have not reached that comfort zone here on earth that most seem to have found in this new gospel that God said 98% are living in a false sense of security not knowing in these last days what is about to come upon them. In retrospect, I can say; I suffered the loss of all things to find God. In view of my experiences, it appears that I may repeat this again to remain on my present course.

It took a tragic divorce to get my attention to save me from myself to serve God in his sovereign will. With no hope of regaining reconciliation with my first wife, God's patience waited for me another fifth-teen years. God walked me into his perfect will through my present wife who He was going to use to bring me to this present state spiritually.

It took seven years to restore me in my spirit after that encounter with the devil. Through this second marriage, I was being preserved for my calling as an **end-time messenger**. One evening while I was sitting in my basement study … my wife was attending a local Assembly of God Church and asked me would I like to go with her one morning, she had not only become my means of stability in my flesh but gave me a new a focus to do what I did not do in my first marriage. When I inquired about this second marriage, He just told me to walk upright and be faithful and everything he had planned for me , I would walk into it.

She was not that religious but a good person. It would be after my visitation in my basement office I would begin to get bits and pieces of this revelation. I had not attended an assembly of any kind until she asked me that morning. I was gifted by God with the knowledge of the human body's functions and construction that led me to become a qualified professional as a Registered Medical Technologist & chief Pathologist Assistant to a forensic pathology group. God sent me to a local medical institute like the one I trained in that hired me on the bassist of what I told them and never asked me for my credentials.

I loss my qualification certificates too. That was his first act of favor in blinding the system that caused me to walk into that position of restoration to do what I had been trained to do. When he baptized me in the Holy Spirit and told me that I would walk into everything he had for me. My present wife is the second of these blessings I walked into.

She is a unique woman, I found that God knows how to put a person in your life to serve His purpose in all things in His sovereign will. My background experiences that only God could have rescued me from are the bassist of my present deep convictions.

We were married in December of 88. In the year 2002 God begin to speak to me in a clear voice in my prayer time that began my transition to this place spiritually. Some of you have never heard the gospel that I have been sending you in layers to help you with ears to hear and eyes to see to save yourself from the last of this wicked and untoward end time generation.

I have not had an easy life because I was not blessed with the wisdom that some of you have in my early years … I made many mistakes along the way … outside of the Holy Spirit, my only comfort has been my wife, mother, my biological sister, a daughter by marriage and a dear missionary brother are my close circle in the lord that help bring me this far. He said I would see the glory of his fullness and in the end as a son and that's the day I'm waiting to experience before I get to go home.

Never assume that you are good enough to go to heaven. **Mark 10:18 "(KJV) ¹⁸ And Jesus said unto him, why callest thou me good? there is none good but one, that is, God."** When I came into the knowledge of the truth, I began to examine what pastor's say that keeps you paying tithes to support their kingdom buildings on earth instead of delivering souls into the kingdom of heaven. These here-say teachings that incorporate filler knowledge bordering on imagination that I no longer contribute too. **2 Corinthians 10:5 "(KJV) ⁵ Casting down imaginations, and every high thing that exalteth itself against the knowledge of God, and bringing into captivity every thought to the obedience of Christ;"** Each one of us as a confessing Christian are responsible for your own conversion in saving your soul first and only the real gospel can do that; although God sees our hearts along with those that are poor in spirit, he chooses his vessels through whom he will?

Now brother, when you say real gospel, what do you mean ... isn't all preaching out of the bible the gospel? When Jesus said, **"by the fruit ye shall know them"** I now can see that Satan has some of the best and gifted seminary trained preachers and teachers I have ever seen behind a pulpit. I'm all for education but just like Jesus said ... **1 Corinthians 1:26 "(KJV) ²⁶ For ye see your calling, brethren, how that not many wise men after the flesh, not many mighty, not many noble, are called:"** What he was saying, when he shows up, people get healed delivered and set free with out asking for and offering to get what God has freely given us all just by asking in faith. I say this because I have attended some tent revivals in my past where you had to get in a line to buy these blessings. That's why the unwise virgins' oil ran out. When Christ shows up, you don't return the way you came, at least I didn't.

Now if that is not happening in your assembly, this is what's happening ... **Hebrews 4:2 "(KJV) ² For unto us was the gospel preached, as well as unto them: but the word preached did not profit them, not being mixed with faith in them that heard it."** When Jesus is lifted in his power, purity, and holiness, that's what will happen. **We all!** ... have fallen from the holiness of Christ by not being the example as he gave us in his apostles on the day of Pentecost? This is the prophecy that has come to pass ... **Isaiah 53:6 "(KJV) ⁶ All we like sheep have gone astray; we have turned everyone to his own way; and the LORD hath laid on him the iniquity of us all."** If he is the only God whose unity is in one body that shows no division, how did we ever get to be what we have become as denominations and separate kingdoms, teaching part of the truth?

Many seminary train pastors and teachers are men educated in the fall-a-way of the doctrine; therefore, a great majority practice the principals taught under Jesuits professors to ensure that they just teach the word from a literal logical theology standpoint. It sounds good, preaches well, makes you look smart and will elevate your status in the ministry with credibility among your peers. This is the broad road entry that does not require an ensample to gain knowledge of the word. It injects the thoughts of men and his opinions. This is when hirelings were brought into the church to compete as leaders for the flock. **Job 7:2 "(KJV) ² As a servant earnestly desireth the shadow, and as an <u>hireling</u> looketh for the reward of his work:"** This layer of scripture applies also to educated pastors who are in the ministry for gain of wealth. They are seduced by Satan to take the easy way out. **John 10:12 "(KJV) ¹² But he that is an hireling, and not the shepherd, whose own the sheep are not,** (These are pastors and ministers that claim you as members of their body and take possession of you as their sheep's and because of your lack of knowledge become your idols in the flesh.) **seeth the wolf coming, and leaveth the sheep, and fleeth: and the wolf catcheth them, and scattereth the sheep."** When you must purchase your education, it comes with the mentality of seeking to gain from it the prestige of your sacrifice. The teachings of men brought division into the body; therefore, men begin to interpret God's word with a degree of imaginations by adding his own thoughts, he changed the context to interpret what he thought it meant.

Isaiah 55:8 "(KJV) ⁸ For my thoughts are not your thoughts, neither are your ways my ways, saith the LORD. There are two kinds of Christians, those **born from above** and those **born from below."** The two categories can be distinguished in the fruit of the spirit. Those **born from above** will seek your welfare and not their own. The word through them will be taught and preached with a demonstration of faith, power and with compassion that brings healing and deliverance from these spirits you know not of.

Those **born from below** will come in the name of the lord as hirelings that demonstrate lack of convictions by not having the right spirit. They can have faith in the name and still not know what spirit they are of. I found out when it comes to spiritual things, your pastors are imparting the spirit of **error** or the spirit of **truth**; therefore, the people in your assembly are receiving what's in their pastor. You don't go to the assembly with a closed spirit; therefore, you are open to receive. That's why you are to search behind anyone who say they come in the name of the lord. **John 5:39 "(KJV) ³⁹ Search the scriptures; for in them ye think ye have eternal life: and they are they which testify of me."** That's what they did at a church in Berea when Paul preached to them things out of the scriptures hard to be understood. They search behind him. **(Acts 17:11)** To start a work with out the leading of the lord will not produce fruit that remain. I tried and it did not produce the right kind of spiritual fruit. Many took offence of my no compromise teachings.

I tried twice to start a work and God did not let it come to pass. I later found out that He had not finished with my conversion as to his perfect will for me as a chosen vessel. This brought to light how you can be deceived by operating in his permissive will. **I was call to be a messenger, not a pastor.** He uses me to reveal what you are now reading in a clear voice He gave me ears to hear. I can't claim an office of one of the fivefold graces in **Eph. 4:11-12**. I have learned that if you must explain what office you serve, you probably went ahead of God because he speaks for himself in the office He represents. I have two living wives at the time I am writing this chronicle, therefore, I don't qualify to represent one of these positions in title or else I would become a stumbling block and a reproach to those that know truth. He refers to me as his messenger and uses me as his mouthpiece.

Although I have certain liberties in him, I minister as I'm led. I never asked for an offering because He told me that all I need would be there when the need arise. I lost everything to find God; he not only restored all things double in this life to me, being debt free except for a mortgage, I now am content to live from day to day. Everything I need was given to me including cars. I have no needs that are not supplied because Christ in me has no needs. In most cases, the few churches that invited me to teach was so small, I left them an offering. God did not call me to start a ministry; therefore, I mostly give away what I don't need monetarily like the apostles did. I don't give just to be giving; I give as I am led to give and bless people for their good works and deeds when I encounter them without regards whether they are saved or sinner. This we do in secret towards God. Many of us without knowing are strengthening the hands of the devil by lack of knowledge in our giving. My faith is in Christ and him being in me, I can witness he's more than able to supply his own needs.

I am content at what state I'm in. I'm only just here for a few days in the flesh compared to eternity. I have more that I need as his child by doing things his way. You see my beloved; I am living in the last of my days on this Earth. When I found out, I had sins of omission in my life on my day of visitation; I began to work on what I needed to do to save myself if I wanted to live for eternity with him.

That visitation put me onto the straight path, I had been a confessing Christian for thirty years from 1972 to 2002 on my way to hell living in a way that seemed right but did not know it. That was my wake-up call to the sins of omission. We, in this last generation are at the end of two parallels; we are going to have to suffer what the early church went through to bring back the gospel and 98% of confessing Christians are not ready to leave this world yet. They are like the people in the days of Noah; buying, selling, getting, and gaining, marrying, giving in marriage, and looking to gain more stuff. Even some of you on my mail list take these messages passively for granted.

Don't let this word become a witness against you? I ask God to give me detailed words to speak and write so there will be no misunderstanding of what I have been trying to communicate to you. This is my personal testimony of a man that stumbled through most of his life as a fool, the least among men and to have been privileged to be given this opportunity to serve him in his perfect will at this late stage in my life that I have found worth dying for. I have a from of dyslexia that caused me to read at a third-grade level. God gave me something so unique as a gift, in spite of this mental handicap, I was gifted with the knowledge of the human body and how it works. I knew where every organ was located and how to remove it surgically from an autopsy point of view. That was a gift that walked me into becoming a certified lab technician. God helped me pass that test.

I know now what it's like to have real joy that the world didn't give me, peace that surpass my understanding, love that I would lay down my life to give you the same opportunity to know the "GREAT I AM" as I have come to know him. He is **"The Same God Yesterday Today and Forever."** So be blessed my beloved, Dr. Martin Luther King said this before he was taken out by evil men, I too have been privileged to look over the mountain top and what I saw leaves me no hope for this world in its present state. Now you know why I am looking forward to the day to be absent from this body and be present with the lord for eternity.

What I have been trying to do in love for your soul, is to share with you something to consider as to who is going to be your judge in the end and tell you what he is going to be requiring of all. We all are going to have to repent that haven't heard or received this vision of our times. Fall on your knees and do what I did after thirty years in error; repent. I am criticized for not belonging to an assembly because I found out that when God open my eyes, I also saw the state of the church. It was then I began to activate the Holy Spirit to teach me how to deliver myself. Nothing I do in self will prosper with fruit that remain;

that I knew from my past. The New Testament Church is in you, led by the Holy Spirit, will give God all the glory. You are the two in the earth that agrees with the father and the son in heaven as touching this gospel where he leads is having church and these signs shall follow them that believe. We are now living in part truths as touching the gospel, operating in separate kingdoms until Christ returns to restore our fallen state back to one body and take us home.

All during this time after the church fell into denominational divisions, the elects are what's holding back the judgment. That is our state whether you believe it or not … **Matthew 24:22 "(KJV) ²² And except those days should be shortened, there should no flesh be saved: but for the elect's sake those days shall be shortened."** The reason why we judge one-another, is because of the doctrines that cause this separation and division among us as confessing Christians, is greatly the work of the Jesuit order of the Catholic Church. They built the seminaries that infiltrated and re-indoctrinated Christianity.

It started with Constantine's introduction of pagan gods to Christianity. Given generations of these doctrines, men with out knowing, became the masters of their own kingdoms just by one error, injected into the real doctrine of Jesus Christ, man's intellect along with keeping pagan practices that shows he still don't know who his god is.

Beloved, you may not have to go through what I did as God deals with your heart. God cause me to give up all to get to this place, so I would have the convictions and faith to speak the word reserved for this generation. I can't fully comprehend the full scope of what he has given me to know. I only know that my past no longer occupies my thoughts. Now I know what Paul meant when he said he was **"forgetting those things behind and reaching forth for those things above"**. We are all going to die at the appointed time; the question is **what state you are in at that time.** We don't want to think about this reality fact of life. Sadly, I have met some that don't believe theirs is a God.

We all have an inborn mentality to want to live forever. That's what came when God brought life to Adam and when he sinned; we are all now born in that state. This shadow of darkness has us under a grand delusion until we are born from above again. It's unfortunate that some of us are still living in that state of delusion as confessing Christians. This I didn't know until he brought me to life with a choice to live with Him for eternity. Now I am in waiting to come out of this wilderness as a John the Baptist messenger of these last days.

The lord is going about in the earth choosing whom he will use so be careful not to defile yourself by speaking evil of each other. Show the love that looks beyond each other's faults and as much as possible, learn to follow peace among yourselves. AMEN

Now on the national front

Our government has been infiltrated by spies in the camp that came in the Trump administration. These are the men that have international ties that connect them with this New World Order. We now see disclosed in these investigations to the point that they can not disclose the full scope of this covert national security breach to the public that Wikileaks and Edward Snowden brought to light.

This is a new supercomputer shared by the NSA and the CIA and Interpol that went online after "911". It was designed to keeps tabs not only on suspected terrorist but private citizens also. It is linked to all, smart TV's, smart phones, Apple and Samsung tablets. They are gold sim cards, chips that are removable or built into the latest above devises that the government requires to link them to this supercomputer. Hacker's now have these sim card codes. The upgrade to this system has already been implemented that can not be hacked and will fully be implemented in the cashless system.

That's why President Trump, a former conspiracy theorist, is trying to discredit the media by coining the phrase **"Fake News."** The New World Order people are some of these billionaires appointed by President Trump. Therefore, Washington is in a leadership gap in these non- political appointments to essential departments of Government. Russia and China are taking advantage of this corrupt government by their covert spies planted in place to leak our security secrets through government private contractors with high level security clearances to get covert code information to these foreign hackers. These sensitive documents will compromise our national security. Donald Trump's presidency tapped into this vacuum of discontentment of the people and became their spokesman. All of this was in God's prophetic plan.

The people of this nation are under judgment for legalizing sodomy, provoked God to transfer the judgment from Obama and brought in Donald Trump to show the extent of high-level corruption in business and government. He will become their instrument of our final destruction economically; being a cymbal of business corruption and immorality as our president, became the voice of blind evangelical patriot Christians. God has given the people what they asked for that represents our moral and social priorities. The majority states with the help of the Electoral College put him in office, not the popular vote. He now will become their fall guy at the hands of his bold ignorance of not knowing the type of people he is dealing with, will be our downfall. He poses no threat to them as being the perfect man in office as their patsy. That's what presidents have become to them that are in control. That's why he is still in campaign mode when he speaks to the people. This is his application of the art of the deal in his business dealings.

Adam and Eve, the War for Gender Supremacy

"The mystery of the beast with-in"

Most of us take evil for granted because we are born into its nature with no knowledge of the degree of control it has over us. Men and women who get to read this chronicle; I desire that you give it much thought as using it to examine yourselves. Eve was the second of God's creation to disobey him and the first in the Earth. Now I want you to keep this in mind because both male and female genders will be given equal time in this exposé of these evils as to how they will be used after the fall.

First, they were joined together by God; **second,** they were of each other as one as created in the natural to become spiritual being. They were as angels in their natural spiritual state with no knowledge of sexual differences; angels are sexless as spiritual beings. God in his foreknowledge of all things created from him these two parts of himself, set the stage for what would be the fall of all species created as male and female including his image mates, Adam and Eve. The question is why did he create them male and female? **Isaiah 46:10 "(KJV) [10] Declaring the end from the beginning, and from ancient times the things that are not yet done, saying, My counsel shall stand, and I will do all my pleasure:"** This is God's foreknowledge that would set the stage for sin to run it's course when they exercise their free will to choose the course of their life. Eve being of Adam made her a co-companion as his comforter being one in spirit. She is the other part of himself that will be able to reproduce his and her images by his seeds from God's DNA in him. Her place as the weaker vessel will not become known until she wonders off from her covering and listens to another voice other than God or her husband. **1 Peter 3:7 "(KJV) [7] Likewise, ye husbands, dwell with them according to knowledge, giving honour unto the wife, as unto the weaker vessel, and as being heirs together of the grace of life; that your prayers be not hindered."**

There's no mention of the women as the weaker vessel in the beginning. These are my Enoch moment to explain the historical significance surrounding these events in dispensational history, as revealed by the Holy Spirit. This part of her nature, having a free will, we are not created to be robots. You see, God's love and ways are beyond our level of knowledge to comprehend. Eden was a testing environment to see how they were going to use something in them they were not aware of; freedom to choose who to serve.

Women, don't take this offensively, your curiosity is that weaker part of your nature that is the reason why God made them male and female; for them to live in harmony, they must walk as one in God's love that will give them the ability look beyond their faults. Only God knows who your rib mate is. Adam is the image of God; therefore, he has the greater responsibility as the Godhead, that's why he carries the seed that creates and duplicates himself through Eve. That's why he is answerable to his creator as an earthly priest. They were equals as one in the garden as the two that became one that lacked no natural needs.

They were free to roam and do whatever God told them and eat whatever they wanted in the garden with one exception; this would be their test. **Genesis 2:9 "(KJV) ⁹ And out of the ground made the LORD God to grow every tree that is pleasant to the sight, and good for food; <u>the tree of life</u> also in the midst of the garden, and the tree of knowledge of good and evil. Genesis 2:17 (KJV) ¹⁷ But of the <u>tree of the knowledge</u> of good and evil, thou shalt not eat of it: for in the day that thou eatest thereof thou shalt surely die."** Now let's see what they had at their disposal that causes them not to have to work or have any lack or need. This is how God does things for his children that at that time didn't require faith because all their provisions were provided for in their spiritual state because God had no needs. They were the first to be born from above as fully created adult children when he breathes upon them. They became His man-children.

I want you to catch a vision at this point; after the fall, you would need faith in God to get those provisions from the enemy who now will take possession of them and become the enemy of your soul from with-in. God made man to be the dominant leader with dominion authority as his priestly image, represented his presents in the earth. Therefore, Eve was to follow him as her lord in the earth together as one wherever they went in the garden. She was of him as his counterpart and comforter. That's what God set in motion before the foundation of the world that can not be changed. **Matthew 19:6 "(ASV) ⁶ So that they are no more two, but one flesh. What therefore God hath joined together, let not man put asunder."**

This is what changed the course of all creation that would cause them to turn on each other. One evening, Eve decided to leave her husband's side and go on a curiosity mission right to the tree of forbidden fruit of the knowledge of good and evil; now of all the trees, why did she decide to go to that one? Guess who was waiting for this moment to get back into the earth; Satan, disguised as a serpent. You see, in Satan's case, this was the only three that had a curse on it; that's why he was there. Here is a holy woman about to have a conversation with an unholy being and be deceived by her own curiosity, by being filled with lies. Look ladies, he is very smooth with an appealing enticing conversation, feeding our conversation because Satan knew she wouldn't be there if not for that reason. This will be the pattern that will run its course through-out history. **Hosea 4:6 "(KJV) ⁶My people are destroyed for lack of knowledge: because thou hast rejected knowledge, I will also reject thee, that thou shalt be no priest to me: seeing thou hast forgotten the law of thy God, I will also forget thy children."** This is the dialogue that led to her being violated in the spirit. **Genesis 3:1-6 "(KJV) ¹Now the serpent was more subtil than any beast of the field which the LORD God had made. And he said unto the woman, Yea, hath God said, Ye shall not eat of every tree of the garden?** (He used the truth to get her attention.) **²And the woman said unto the serpent, We may eat of the fruit of the trees of the garden: ³But of the fruit of the tree which is in the midst of the garden, God hath said, Ye shall not eat of it, neither shall ye touch it, lest ye die.** (Now that Satan has her attention, the truth will now be twisted into a lie in a way that would peak her curiosity into enticement.) **⁴And the serpent said unto the woman, Ye shall not surely die: ⁵For God doth know that in the day ye eat thereof, then your eyes shall be opened, and ye shall <u>be as gods,</u>** (Notice the small "g" … after this act is completed in her , Satan will now speak through her in order to become the god of this world, Adam with knowing will be giving up all that God gave him to rule over when he act on the word of this condemned angel.) **knowing good and evil. ⁶And when the woman saw that the tree was good for food, and that it was pleasant to the eyes, and a tree to be desired to make one wise, she took of the fruit thereof, and did eat,** (Satan represents sin and by her talking to him, his sin nature is appealing to her free will thoughts, activating her nature that is attracted to sin; the flesh. The lust of the eye the lust of the flesh and the prides of life and she yields to act, this is her sin.) **and gave also unto her husband with her; and he did eat."** Adam had the responsibility not to hear anyone but God's voice, Satan enters Eve as the evil now with-in without her even knowing what she had done. In her (Eve) he speaks to Adam. Disobedience has consequences, they saw each other naked for the first time and hid themselves in shame and fear. Now God comes down in the cool of the evening to have his daily talk with Adam and he does not greet him as usual. This is the voice that was distinguished as the one he knew from that one he had acted on that caused him to fear. **Genesis 3:10-13 "(KJV) ¹⁰ And he said, I heard thy voice in the garden, and I was afraid, because I was naked; and I hid myself.** (Adam knew the voice of God. Now for the first time, he feared God.) **¹¹ And he said, who told thee that thou wast naked? Hast thou eaten of the tree, whereof I commanded thee that thou shouldest not eat? ¹² And the man said, The woman whom thou gavest to be with me, she gave me of the tree, and I did eat.** (This was man's first act of not excepting responsibility for his actions but rather blamed God for giving him that woman.) **¹³ And the LORD God said unto the woman, what is this that thou hast done? And the woman said, the serpent beguiled me, and I did eat."**

This is that weaker nature in a time of innocence with no knowledge of evil, having a free will to choose. Adam partook also and therefore Satan's plan is now complete. He not only took possession of the two of them, but now can procreate his own children using their corrupt DNA seeds with evil strands of his own DNA that will be used to produce men with megalomania minds with a god like superiority complexes.

Eve was the first act of disobedience as the weaker vessel in the Earth. After the resurrection of Christ, another woman representing her fall into immorality, will witness the new Adams resurrection and carry the first message of her redemption to his disciples; Mary Magdalene. Now women, she was carrying a message not to peach a sermon. When Adam sinned, he set in motion things that throughout times, ages, and dispensations would set in motion a sin course that would be completed after six thousand years. The time in between will be sin running its course to bring the world back to the first millennium conditions before the fall.

All biblical history from Noah to this present day is prerecorded in the mystery of the prophet's visions of time, ages and dispensations to be interpreted by revelation knowledge to man and persuade him to return to his creator. Throughout this time ... **2 Timothy 3:13 "(KJV) ¹³ But evil men and seducers shall wax worse and worse, deceiving, and being deceived."** There are doctrines that teach all are going to heaven because we can't live perfect in this world because of sin. That's because they have left Jesus out of their doctrine. God moves in the spirit in the earth selecting souls he as predestined in the book of life to live with him for eternity. He reveals himself through his elects and those who receive them make their calling and election sure.

The traditions of the Christian church have put the Holy Ghost in the pew to contain him so they can have some structure and order in their assemblies as to help God win souls the way man thinks it should be done. Therefore, History in the gentile age will be repeated. **Mark 7:9 "(KJV) ⁹ And he said unto them, Full well ye reject the commandment of God, that ye may keep your own tradition."** What man released without knowing is an unholy Ghost that will fill the house with all seven of these religious spirits in one body in Revelation two that will give place to these sins of omission by not knowing what spirit you are of or have become. He will be … **2 Timothy 3:7 "(ASV) ⁷ ever learning, and never able to come to the knowledge of the truth."**

This will become a carnal assembly worshipping in flesh. This is where gender competition will now compete for authority over each other by exploiting each other's weaknesses and faults. The rising of the Jezebel spirit. This is what happen in the book of Revelation at the church in the spirit of **Thyatira** that use the female gender to take advantage of men leaders who were becoming weak to the point of allowing their wives to have a voice in the male stead in the assembly. This is where they begin to teach the men and throughout time as they gained followers, they appointed themselves as pastors; therefore, violating God's rule of order in the assembly. They will operate in the permissive will of God.

This has put the church the apostles set up as Paul instructed Timothy does not deviate from. **Revelation 2:20 "(KJV) ²⁰ Notwithstanding I have a few things against thee, because thou sufferest that woman Jezebel, which calleth herself a prophetess,** (In this context a pastor.) **to teach and to seduce my servants to commit fornication, and to eat things sacrificed unto idols."** (This is what caused Solomon to fall from God's favor by letting his wives seduce him to compromise God's commandments by serving other gods. This will be the test of your true convictions as the male image of God.) **1 Timothy 2:12 "(KJV) ¹² But I suffer not a woman to teach, nor to usurp authority over the man, but to be in silence."** I must interject at this point; it was twenty-five years into my second marriage when she began to tell others I was her Abraham. Charity begins at home, If the God I serve is real, then I set out to prove that there's nothing too hard that he can't change. In order for her to become my Eve I had to become Adam as the God man in her life. He proved His word to me that took twenty-five years to fulfill.

This is what got me put out of my hometown churches when I said I could not find a scripture context to justify God took Adam's head and put it on Eve when he fail. Women may be used to prophecy but her primary calling is to teach women to women ministry just as I see **Joyce Meyer** is doing in this time. I have learned to see the good being done in the right where sincerity of heart is concern. It is not my place to judge another man's servant. I have watch her grow spiritually over the years as I have and see she has maintained per place in the ministry given her.

As women, you are to be the holy version of Eve restored. The married women are to teach the younger married and single women how to conduct themselves among the male gender as to not tempt them. They play a very important role in a man's life when they are joined together as one; then they are equals that know their place in the order of God's kingdom. We all have fallen short by not having a Godly example with convictions that point you to the father, not man. I have seen too many confessing Christian women whose children have gone astray by neglecting to train them by example the way they should go as a confessing Christian mother. She is a helpmate to the man to build him up and not to speak evil of him in public. Now tell me, is there anyone in your life as a fellow confessing brother or sister with convictions that would sacrifice their friendship with you before they would compromise standing on the truth?

This is what I was shown in my re-teaching by the Holy Ghost to show how far we all have fallen including me. This is where I concluded; we all have missed it except for those he elected to keep his presence in the earth to make their calling and election sure. Therefore, pastors don't deal with the third layer in these books of Peter, Ephesians, Timothy and the Corinthian letters as to the deep truth that will keep the devil's jezebel spirits be it male or female from taking over your assemblies. This spirit use gender to its own advantage. I was told years ago before I was divorced that you can't build a church teaching hard truth like this. Many have departed from me since I came into my divine calling as a messenger.

This teaching will test your marriage and if you were not joined by God. If I had been taught this in my first encounter with salvation, I could have saved my marriage. When the Holy Spirit taught me this, I put God to the test by faith in his word because I didn't want to lose a second time. **1 Corinthians 7:16 "(KJV) ¹⁶ For what knowest thou, O wife, whether thou shalt save thy husband? or how knowest thou, O man, whether thou shalt save thy wife? 1 Corinthians 7:15 (ASV) ¹⁵ Yet if the unbelieving departeth, let him depart: the brother or the sister is not under bondage in such cases: but God hath called us in peace."**

That's why I had to become my second wife's Abraham to win her the right way. Your Judas might be lying beside you in bed. It has come to my attention that those that are called with these convictions are having to make some hard decisions that are costing some relationships in marriage to be in jeopardy as many are being tried as to their loyalties by their choices. I found out that my priority first is my home where I am to become a priest and her Abraham. This I did in my second marriage that came with four mature daughters and one son.

I have two sons of my first marriage. In my second marriage, I presented myself as a man that not only loved their mother but respected them as young women. When my biological son from my first marriage met them, they treated him as their brother in love. Now you know why I speak with such convictions. Although they think I'm one of a kind, there are more; we are the few that walk like this. This is how I got to know God through his word. My life has always been one trial after another. I used God's fruits to help me die by judging my action by his fruit. If the way I acted did not match His fruit, I just repented when I saw myself wrong. God will teach you how to love and live in peace under the most difficult circumstances if you can humble yourself. That's what happens when you seek first his kingdom, and he will work all things out to your good. This is what the Holy Ghost spoke through Peter on the day of Pentecost about saving yourself first. **(Acts 2:39)**

In our present state of apostasy, pastors and spiritual leaders in darkness and with their own agendas have caused us by lack of faith in the doctrine the apostles preached, send us to hospitals and mental institution for not having the conviction to pay the price to let Christ do what he said he would do if we believed him. The first church in oneness was the hospital and mental institutions where sickness, diseases and demon were cast out. That's why I keep telling you that we all are going to have to repent for being so divided that caused this unbelief where the world can't see Jesus in the assemblies that name his name.

It took me thirty years to get to this win-win situation to keep the devil off of me; as to say, to live is to be in the lord, to die is to gain eternal life. I strive to live with-in this hope; that's why I had to let everything go in my past and deny myself of things I desired but had to let go to see my future in heaven. When the fruit remains in you, God will use you to produce that fruit in others as an ensample of himself that it may remain in them. Then and only then is he lifted. I must admit; I find myself always living on the edge of gain and lost in my determination to stand on the convictions the Holy Spirit has taught me.

It is the responsibility of every believer to have this type of relation with Christ. You see, I'm dyslexic and read at a third-grade level with a good memory. This work is of the Holy Ghost in me. All throughout grade school, I was often humiliated when I had to read. As one of the class dummies, God help me pass my MT board's exam after four years of training at a well-known research institution in New York that qualified me for what he had gifted me to do. I walked into my profession. If God can use me like he did those disciples as some were ignorant unlearn men; well, I'm in good company. I could not get anyone to take the time to edit my writing and I wondered why. The king James Bible is an unedited version of in-correct English; **"the people that read what I give to you to say will already have ears to hear it."** As an intercessor, I'm warring in the spirit daily for souls I have never seen but God knows them and that's all that matters.

It cost me all to find God and if I must pay that cost to keep him again, to him be the glory. I am waiting for my day to give him the glory he so richly deserves for all he has done for an unworthy nobody like me. I don't grieve over the loses along the way … he has given me great comfort in taking the hurts away. Though in my striving, I came short so many times and so have many of you when I tried to help him by not understanding.

I want to be as transparent as I can to show you what deliverance look like when you can only see what God has done and not you. Don't let pride be your sin of omission that get you judged as the devil's child. I am testifying of him. All I have left is his strength; I look forward to my day of redemption. I requested one last thing of him to let me experience him in the fullness of his glory at my departure time like Deacon Stephen whose name I bare. I want to be able to give him the same glory in my death.

Inquiry explanations expanded.

Recently, I was asked to explain further about the beast in connection with the internet. I revealed in time past how the mysteries of the bible speak in **twos** and **threes**. The bible is written to the Jew and the Gentile believers under grace and truth; **that's the twos.**

The threes are the layers of the word that reveal the full mystery revelations that when you seek ask and knock will be unlocked according to the times, age and the dispensation as to what applies in that time to be revealed.

Isaiah 28:13 "(KJV) [13] But the word of the LORD was unto them precept upon precept, precept upon precept; line upon line, line upon line; here a little, and there a little; that they might go, and fall backward, and be broken,

and snared, and taken." God knew man down through time would fall victim of things unknown to him by his own willing ignorance that trust in his carnal environment of the senses.

The whole council of the word is in the complete three layers which is the revelation of Jesus Christ as revealed in the one new man coming out of the volume of the books of the bible. This mystery is found in this verse … **2 Thessalonians 2:7 "(KJV) ⁷ For the mystery of iniquity doth already work: only he who now letteth will let, until he be taken out of the way."**

This now is the work of the angel Michael, restraining the activity of the devil throughout these dispensations to control the activity of demon spirits from infringing upon God's timetable. God created Satan; therefore, he is the only one that can contain him. This scripture is the manifestation of the third layer of this mystery revelation. … **Ephesians 2:2 "(KJV) ² Wherein in time past ye walked according to the course of this world, according to the <u>prince of the power of the air</u>, the spirit that now worketh in the <u>children of disobedience</u>:"**

When Nebuchadnezzar saw the stature of the beast man, it was both literal and spiritual that held the mystery of the times that would be revealed in the stages of kingdoms and governments that would become wickedly evil throughout time as Daniel's interpretation of the dream. The **first** layer is Satan as a spirit operating in the earth in kingdoms. The **second** layer is him operating in man. The **third layer** is him operating as a AI (Artificial Intelligence) the beast system as the ten toes in the last days coming through the airwaves to take total control of man's mind. You see, in the time of grace, everything is spiritual; therefore, this beast of our time will be a spiritual manifestation of mind control by way of the airwaves that will be literally held in not be human but exercise authority over your mind with the ability to speak.

Satan had to be restrained. When the watcher angels came to the daughters of men, **(Gen. 6:2)** this was the mixing of heavenly DNA with man's earthly DNA; when manifested, would become the forbidden zone of knowledge that will infringe upon God's timeline by carrying the presence of this superior strand of heavenly DNA in the earth.

We now are about to enter the ten toes of Nebuchadnezzar's dream when our economy collapses. This will be Satan's last stand to manifest in man what caused the flood. The use of this forbidden angelic DNA to control the world will be introduced through the airwaves we will come to know as the internet. America, the Modern Babylon, will introduce to the world the ability to communicate with each other in their own native language; this is Babylon of old returned through the technology that will bring the revelation of this third layer of the **"prince of the power of the air." (Eph. 2:2)** Steve Jobs will be the carrier of this forbidden DNA knowledge that will bring Apple to the forefront of dominance with this technology.

It is no accident but by design a demonic manifestation that will be a sign to God's prophets and messengers when this appears. He will use this cymbal of a bite out of an apple as his trademark. (**Forbidden fruit**) This is going to be the sign to the elects that he was going to be the one that become the major player among these megalomaniacs to be instrumental in causing the crossover into the new time continuum when he introduces his smart i-phone as the beast that speaks.

What we are now experiencing in the world at this present time is the disruption of time brought on by using this forbidden knowledge. Steve Jobs knew he was special by having this superior Gene that gave him this ability. He and Bill Gates will become the techno giants of this time but separate because of their genius abilities. Satan came through the airwaves in the introduction of the internet as a spirit to begin to captivate the minds of the whole world. When we realize this before the tribulation, this is what we will appear to be spiritually … **Revelation 12:9 "(KJV) ⁹And the great dragon was cast out, that old serpent, called <u>the Devil, and Satan, which deceiveth the whole world</u>: he was cast out into the earth, and his angels were cast out with him."** Once this was accomplished, now all he had to do is deliver the means to control each mind individually; in comes Steve Jobs, with this strand of DNA that not only would discover and decode the wavelength to your brainwaves but write the algorisms code that will decode your brain's fingerprint wavelength individually.

All civilizations or tribes who infringed upon the use of this knowledge in time past were destroyed. This was the work of Ark angel Michael restraining them. Steve Jobs, with all his billions, died of an incurable cancer when he introduced it. He transferred this technology to his head counterpart that introduced it in i-phone six and enhance it in i-phone ten. If you have an apple phone, it has been automatically upgraded. They brought back in a modern revamped version of the Pokémon game to test it; that's when you saw all these people converging in public places with-out knowing why.

They were post hypnotically sent there by this app when they opened it on their phone. This is evidence of how you will be marked in the spirit. That's why people with Apple i-phones can't live without them. This is the same code that cause you to upgrade each time a new product is introduced. When people were complaining of the phones being slow, this is a program to get you to purchase a new one. This is a sign of how you will be marked by the beast without even knowing what spirit possessed you because you would become the prisoner of this beast.

On the National Front, our Countries State

Recently, the events that lead up to the election of President Donald Trump as I watched the activities of this president as they unfold in biblical history to avoid making statements regarding my own opinion. It is my desire to see what God sees. As a watcher of **"God's news behind the news,"** it is evident that spiritual forces of international origin are at work to deceive our government.

When God gave Israel over to her enemies for turning against him, it came in the form of a delusion to blind their decision making. I see the same scenarios at work in the spirit world that delivered Israel into the hands of her enemies has now returned in our time as history repeating itself. To understand what I'm about to reveal to you, you must see things as history repeating itself biblically. In that last chronicle, I wrote about how I discovered the bible speaking in twos and threes. The twos represent the two nations chosen by God to deal with throughout times, ages and dispensations: Israel, his chosen and the Gentiles, Christ's body under grace and truth. The events we see literally are the transition signs to the tribulation of the Earth's second stage of restoration. God set all these things in motion before the world begin. **(Isa 46:10)**

Therefore, we are about to experience what has already happen before, just in another dispensation of time. It's the gentile's time to suffer that same fate as did their predecessor Israel. The new time continuum is about to be set to transcend into the last millennium. This period is known as the tribulation of man and the Earth which will be over a seven-year period. My chronicle book, **"Revelation; The final layer revealed"** explains the transition of the events leading up to the new millennium.

I am providing you with a background to help you not only see but understand the dilemma we as a gentile free born nation of people find ourselves that we are not prepared mentally to except. We have chosen to be willingly ignorant as our current position in world affairs; as its policeman, have now rendered ourselves helpless with no dignified way out but by war. Under the new administration, our national pride will now be the means of our downfall. The reason, God said ... **Proverbs 16:18 "(ASV) [18] Pride goeth before**

destruction, And a haughty spirit before a fall." It is the way the devil will deceive you into making you think you are right and lead you into his trap that guarantees you will fall in his hands. Those that are under the influence of this delusion will believe what they are doing is right ... **Proverbs 16:25 "(ASV)** [25] **There is a way which seemeth right unto a man, But the end thereof are the ways of death."** That's why Paul prayed for every believer to have discernment. The actions of this president are certainly questionable as to our direction as a nation.

About the stock market

Our economy is about to collapse because of fighting two wars and hear we are about to create the conditions for the third and final war. The rise of the stock market will be a false bubble to catch many in it's sudden overnight fall. This time, we will not recover because those behind the New World Order have planned it that way. Some of the most respected stock advisors are telling you to buy, anticipating this bubble and think that they are smart enough to predict at what point to sale when great profits can be gained in this bubble. This time, without knowing, God will catch them all in His break and prove them wrong. We are a nation under a delusion with the curse of Sodom and Gomorrah upon us as decreed under the Obama administration. This blindness not to see that we are a nation about to default and all we must show is this blind pride. With all this corruption with-in, think we have the means to pull this off and recover?

I spoke this without knowing the outcomes of the election of Donald Trump, don't speak evil of the man you might succeed as president, you may become the one to take the fall of all the others' that have contributed to this in history. Donald Trump reflects the delusion we are under as a nation inhabited of every foul spirit. These are spirits loosed to captivate the minds of people whose brainwaves are linked into this **matrix** of a non-realistic view of reality of the condition we find ourselves. This includes all religions that have departed from the apostle's doctrine in favor of patriotism to country and practice the inclusion of these pagan gods.

We are drunk with power and staggering into and abyss we created. We are now ruled by a hand-held device that controls how we interact with each other. Our love has turned cold with the use of these non-personal interactions by the use of these AI devices. We can ruin each other's lives just by tapping a few keys on a computer. Godless people do godless things with no regard for human life because part of us is blind to our humanity. That's that inward part of you that cause Cain possessed with a murdering demon to literally kill his own brother

Abel. That's what we are capable of doing when we are provoked to the point to expose the manifestation of these hidden evils from with-in. Psychiatrists call them crimes of passion. This is a form of momentary insanity where this spirit that is capable of murder is activated by certain degrees of extreme inward anger that create this condition with-in some of us, activate this dark spirit that caused you not to know what made you do it.

That's why we need to be delivered completely from these spirits we know not of. Satan had to get deliverance out of the church that cause all these spirits to be cast out at the word spoken at the command of the Holy Spirit. America, being a nation founded in a Christian heritage, is targeted by Satan just as Israel; God's chosen. This is the battle in your mind for those who stand to inherit these blessings of divine authority and protection.

I strive to condense these messages to the point as the ministry of the Holy Spirit to bring you a well-informed background of how we got to be like this and why we all need to repent. If Jesus came to his own and they didn't recognize him as their Messiah, having been given the law direct from God to study along with the prophets to inform them of the consequences of their actions and they fail to keep it. Do you think He is going to wink on our willing ignorance? Here we are was as gentiles trying to impose the law on us gentiles that Jews couldn't keep by trying to mix law and grace together and think people are going to see Christ in the spirit. Here we are at the end of the gentile's time, being judged as confessing Christians, not being able to recognize his voice because we have been made to think we are spiritual while yet carnal in our actions. Imposing the law in error in the time of grace and truth. If the Jews couldn't keep it in their time of the law, what is it that made you think that you are better than they and they had a long history to get it right. Speaking this kind of truth is what got the prophet kill by their own people they were sent to save. No doubt, this may come as an offence to some of you who practice a form of the law as a doctrine with out mercy or love. Now do you see how history is repeated in the bible for this reason … **Ecclesiastes 1:9 "(ASV) [9] That which hath been is that which shall be; and that which hath been done is that which shall be done: and there is no new thing under the sun. John 15:20 (ASV) [20] Remember the word that I said unto you, A servant is not greater than his lord. If they persecuted me, <u>they will also persecute you;</u> if they kept my word, they will keep yours also."** I have provided this on background to help you see the delusional state of our leadership from church divisions to government divisions; now can you see the parallels? We now have a president that shows signs of being doubleminded and unstable in his decision making by not following national and international protocols. He has been allowed to get away will breaking constitutional laws by having a corrupt political appointed Supreme Court and a legislative body that acts along party lines with no regards for what's good for the Republic but stands as a corrupt Republican and Democratic party who now, through blind guides, will deliver us all into political hell. Leaders in the House and Senate legislating, changing the laws as needed to suit their political agendas of this hidden government. What we have here is a failure to communicate, as a Modern version of Rome, we are about to witness a major fall from with-in. The corruption from the president all the way down to our local government's actions will guide us right into hands of our enemies through blind pride. His dictator personality may have good intentions but at the wrong time in history. The only thing that will restrain him, are the prayers the saints.

All these Middle Eastern tribes are motivated by the teachings of various forms of their Koran just as many Christian churches are motivated with patriot Christian beliefs contrary to biblical teachings. The Klue Klux Klan are confessing Christians that killed people of color by hanging them in the name of white supremacy. Extreme factions of Muslim teaching told them to behead all who do not believe in their way of life. This is religious madness taking advantage of mindless men to produce religious fools that will turn him against his own brothers to do what Cain did to Abe; kill us all in the name of their god. What we have today is a result of what Sarah used to influence her husband the same way Eve did with her husband, by getting Abraham to lay with Hagar and now they are here in great numbers all over the world, fighting among themselves and killing anyone who gets in their way to claim an illegitimate birth-rite.

These things were written for our learning but only those born from above will be given the revelation to save yourself in your short time here on Earth. **(John 6:44)** When President Trump ordered that strike as a retaliatory act to an incident that did not happen on our soil, he overstepped the NATO alliance. This is the pride of being a self-appointed policeman of the world. Without knowing, we are being set up by forces of evil that got us into these wars by false intelligence to be the catalyst to start the third world war. One thing in my analysis of these last two presidents, Obama considered the consequences of the first gassings that happen on Syrian soil and used a diplomatic approach. Assad realized at that time from the response of the world and NATO, willingly gave up the weapons of mass destruction or be the target of his own demise. Let me provide you with spiritual insight behind this incident? These war hungry politicians in our Congress open the door for this deception that led to getting caught up into another Middle East war. Do you not think that

Isis could not get their hands on this gas and a plane to deliver it on Syrian soil? They used us to take out that base for them. They know by us using what they know about our own spy technology in the sky? They learned that from drone attacks. Our satellites saw where the plane came from, they already know about the rational behavior of our current president, played right into their hands. He didn't even have to get the approval of the Congress because the mood in Washington was to give the president some political points to improve his image. No one brought charges to show how he violated the Constitutional War Powers Act by not consulting congress. These acts of aggression were not committed on our soil or against us as a nation. God knew in these last days these people would destroy themselves along with any nation that get in their way.

These people are born with an inbred vengeance killing instinct against the Jews for four thousand years; they will kill each other to see who can claim the birth rite tribe all the way to the battle of Amor getting. Russia and the United States destabilized their territories when we committed acts of aggression on their homeland soil. We are being manipulated by people who have studied war strategies and given the present technology we invented, used it to draw us into a war traps. Russia and China are not at all bothered by our actions; God has them on the sideline watching to come in and burry us once we have put the nails in our coffin.

President Assad is not stupid to the point of taking himself out by repeating what he knows would defeat him if he were to do it again. Obama did the right thing diplomatically. President Trump's actions are dictated by the sentiment of the people and a blind House of Representatives who have lost their sense of scruples. He came into office on his terms, and we will be taken out by his defiant ego by not going by established international protocol.

May God have mercy on all that call upon his name? AMEN

The wrath of God; the Mystery of the Seven Thunders

Background Scriptures:

Revelation 10:4 (KJV) ⁴ And when the seven thunders had uttered their voices, I was about to write: and I heard a voice from heaven saying unto me, Seal up those things which the seven thunders uttered, and write them not.

In the book of Revelation, there's no mention of the events of the seven thunders before or after the rapture that we can readily comprehend; there is no mention of the details of the seven thunders as outline in the seals, trumpets and vials; however, it is in the bible. All that is written to the Jews and the Gentiles are contained in the word through the prophets as God's method of warning his chosen under law and grace. When the church is removed in **Rev. 14:15-17**, the works of the Holy Spirit is finished and all the saints will rise in the rapture of the second resurrection, just as those who rose with Jesus in the first.

At that time, the church's final warning from the prophets and messengers, just as they were in the days of Noah and to the Jews, would be in a state of apostasy. In that state, the church at that time will reject their warnings just as Israel did and therefore, history will be repeated. Just as the book of Revelation contain visions John saw in no particular order, it is not written in a discernable order on purpose to conceal its mystery to a church that would be taught to see only one side of God from a loving tiptoe through the tulips point of view. They will be unprepared to receive the other side of God in his wrath state. Therefore, there's no mentions of the thunder details. This revelation was to be taught among the churches through those that remained in the apostle's doctrine where the whole council of the word is given to set you free from all the oppression of the devil including lack of knowledge. Whether you believe this statement or not, it is a fact: we, as Christians in our divided state only know in part until that we missed is returned in the outpouring of the latter rain.

Only God is the judge of who he has received up until that time. **1 Corinthians "13:12 (NASB77) [12] For now we see in a mirror dimly, but then face to face; now I know in part, but then I shall know fully just as I also have been fully known."** When the church is removed, it was to escape the wrath that no one would survive because we will be entering another time continuum and only those chosen to repopulate the millennium will survive. The wrath is reserve for the wicked; that's why the tribulation is to purify the saints to make them whole in the image of Christ to His glory had to be cut short. Now let me remind you of some mysteries the Holy Spirit revealed to me in time past.

First, where or who is the mystery Babylon?

Revelation "17:5 (NASB77) [5] and upon her forehead a name was written, a mystery, " BABYLON THE GREAT, THE MOTHER OF HARLOTS AND OF THE ABOMINATIONS OF THE EARTH." America is the spiritual Mystery Babylon. Explanation: under grace and truth, everything takes on a spiritual meaning. We will invent the internet. It will give the world the capacity to communicate all over the world in real time and be understood in your own languages. This is Modern Babylon; returned through the **"prince of the power of the air;"** Satan coming riding the air waves that will be represented in a non-human entity, the beast. The confirming of her fate when she goes to war by setting her troops on the soil of the Babylon of old, Iraq. She will be setting the stage that will cause history to repeat itself as you see this mystery unfold.

I wrote the sequence of this mystery in the book of **"Revelation"** as the third layer released in two thousand eighteen. Now let's look at the witness the prophet Jeremiah shows of us in the third layer as a witness that reveal what's happening during the silent thunder judgment of the wrath of God as revealed through the eyes of Jeremiah. What he sees will be Israel's siege under Babylonian captivity of old that will be repeated in the last generation of the Gentiles under grace and truth. Only this time, they will be joined by the armies of the North. Yes, Iraq (Babylon of old) is coming back with a vengeance against the Jews, allied with the North.

This is what Jeremiah lamented over in that siege; this is our thunder judgment explained.

Jeremiah 50:1-46 "(NASB77) [1] **The word which the LORD spoke concerning Babylon, the land of the Chaldeans, through Jeremiah the prophet** (this land is now modern Iraq and Iran.) [2] **"Declare and proclaim among the nations. Proclaim it and lift up a standard. Do not conceal it but say, ' Babylon has been captured, Bel has been put to shame,** (Their idols in pride) **Marduk has been shattered; Her images have been put to shame, her idols have been shattered.** (When American troops when to Iraq, one of the first things they did is to remove the modern day statures of the Saddam Husain.) [3] **"For a nation has come up against her out of the north;** (This is their northern invasion by America.) **it will make her land an object of horror,** (This will be the destabilization state we will leave them in, that will contribute to tribal in-fighting for control). **and there will be no inhabitant in it. Both man and beast have wandered off, they have gone away!** (This will be the effect when we are invaded by the armies of the north as did Babylon of Old as Russia, China and the Middle Eastern nation will as the modern Babylon.) [4] **"In those days and at that time," declares the LORD, "the sons of Israel will come, both they and the sons of Judah as well; they will go along weeping as they go, and it will be the LORD their God they will seek.** [5] **"They will ask for the way to Zion, turning their faces in its direction; they will come that they may join themselves to the LORD in an everlasting covenant that will not be forgotten.** (When Israel's time of travail comes in the second half of the tribulation, they will repent as a nation in travail.) [6] **"My people have become lost sheep; Their shepherds have led them astray. They have made them turn aside on the mountains; They have gone along from mountain to hill and have forgotten their resting place.** (This will be their state in their day of visitation.) [7] **"All who came upon them have devoured them; And their adversaries have said, ' We are not guilty, Inasmuch as they have sinned against the LORD who is the habitation of righteousness, Even the LORD, the hope of their fathers.'** [8] **"Wander away from the midst of Babylon, And go forth from the land of the Chaldeans; Be also like male goats at the head of the flock.** (God will cause Israel to not participate in these wars we are fighting because they are designed to bring us into judgment. Israel's primary task is getting ready for their assault in the end.) [9] **"For behold, I am going to arouse and bring up against Babylon A horde of great nations from the land of the north, And they will draw up their battle lines against her; From there she will be taken captive. Their arrows will be like an expert warrior Who does not return empty-handed.** (Their weapons will hit their targets) [10] **"And**

Chaldea will become plunder; (When we invaded Iraq, the destabilization cause near by tribes to plunder and destroy all the great artifacts of Babylon of old; therefore, these armies of the north will plunder this nation when we are invaded.) **All who plunder her will have enough," declares the LORD.** [11] **"Because you are glad, because you are jubilant, O you who pillage My heritage, because you skip about like a threshing heifer and neigh like stallions,** (Our enemies will rejoice at our downfall at the cost of their own stability. [12] **Your mother will be greatly ashamed, she who gave you birth will be humiliated.** (Great Britten has always regarded us as their offspring, they will be sore grieved at our downfall.) **Behold, she will be the least of the nations, A wilderness, a parched land, and a desert.** [13] **"Because of the indignation of the LORD she will not be inhabited, but she will be completely desolate; Everyone who passes by Babylon will be horrified and will hiss because of all her wounds.** [14] **"Draw up your battle lines against Babylon on every side, all you who bend the bow; Shoot at her, do not be sparing with your arrows, for she has sinned against the LORD.** (When the invasion is complete, 70% of all Americans will have been destroyed.) [15] **"Raise your battle cry against her on every side! She has given herself up, her pillars have fallen, her walls have been torn down. For this is the vengeance of the LORD: Take vengeance on her; As she has done to others, so do to her.** [16] **"Cut off the sower from Babylon, And the one who wields the sickle at the time of harvest; From before the sword of the oppressor They will each turn back to his own people, and they will each flee to his own land.** (When the wars begin, all will be directed at America; many will try to return to their home countries.) [17] **"Israel is a scattered flock, the lions have driven them away. The first one who devoured him was the king of Assyria, and this last one who has broken his bones is Nebuchadnezzar king of Babylon.** (Our president as Modern Babylon will dissert Israel; therefore, all nations will turn against her to take her down because we no longer can defend her.) [18] **"Therefore thus says the LORD of hosts, the God of Israel: 'Behold, I am going to punish the king of Babylon and his land,** (This now will become the second wave of God's wrath to Modern Babylon for deserting Israel.) **just as I punished the king of Assyria.** [19] **'And I shall bring Israel back to his pasture, and he will graze on Carmel and Bashan, and his desire will be satisfied in the hill country of Ephraim and Gilead.** [20] **'In those days** (This has reference to Israel's restoration during the tribulation.) **and at that time,' declares the LORD, 'search will be made for the iniquity of Israel, but there will be none; and for the sins of Judah, but they will not be found;** (The tribe of Judah will rise and defend Israel in her travail just as they did by the help of angels in the 1967 war.) **for I shall pardon those whom I leave as a remnant.'** (They are the remnant to repopulate the millennium.) **²¹ "Against the land of Merathaim, go up against it, And against the inhabitants of Pekod. Slay and utterly destroy them," declares the LORD, "And do according to all that I have commanded you. ²² "The noise of battle is in the land, And great destruction.** (This is what's described in the book of Revelation as the battle of Amour Getting now coming against Israel.) **²³ "How the hammer of the whole earth Has been cut off and broken! How Babylon has become an object of horror among the nations!** (We are destroyed in the first half of tribulation during the third world war.) **²⁴ "I set a snare for you, and you were also caught, O Babylon, while you yourself were not aware;** (Our pride that made us the policeman of the world, turned our allies into our enemies when we departed from being the defender of Israel.) **You have been found and also seized Because you have engaged in conflict with the LORD." ²⁵ The LORD has opened His Armory and has brought forth the weapons of His indignation, for it is a work of the Lord GOD of hosts in the land of the Chaldeans.** (Our war with Iraq destabilized that area of the Middle East and cause the remnant tribe of the Chaldeans in Iran to rise and band with the army of the north, Russia.) **²⁶ Come to her from the farthest border; Open her barns, pile her up like heaps and utterly destroy her, let nothing be left to her. ²⁷ Put all her young bulls to the sword;** (They will plunder this nation; the slaughter of our young innocent soldiers during these wars as blood for blood.) **Let them go down to the slaughter! Woe be upon them, for their day has come,**

The time of their punishment. ²⁸ There is a sound of fugitives and refugees from the land of Babylon, (These are the few that escape America in her judgment by rapture) … **To declare in Zion the vengeance of the LORD our God, Vengeance for His temple.** (Those that were martyred for the gospel are referred to as his temples.) **²⁹ "Summon many against Babylon, all those who bend the bow: Encamp against her on every side, let there be no escape. Repay her according to her work; According to all that she has done, so do to her; For she has become arrogant against the LORD, Against the Holy One of Israel.** (We as a nation and a people are being punished for turning against Israel.) **³⁰ "Therefore her young men will fall in her streets, and all her men of war will be silenced in that day,"** (This statement means, many young men will die in battle.) … **declares the LORD. ³¹ "Behold, I am against you, O arrogant one," Declares the Lord GOD of hosts, "For your day has come, the time when I shall punish you. ³² "And the arrogant one** (The president in office at that time will become arrogant toward our allies and in their retaliation, we … **will stumble and fall With no one to raise him up; And I shall set fire to his cities, and it will devour all his environs."** (This is what will happen during the siege of America, the Modern Babylon.) **³³ Thus says the LORD of hosts, "The sons of Israel are oppressed, And the sons of Judah as well; And all who took them captive have held them fast, they have refused to let them go.** (Israel in her former siege was held captive for seventy years.) **³⁴ "Their Redeemer is strong, the LORD of hosts is His name; He will vigorously plead their case, so that He may bring rest to the earth,** God will once again have to come to the aid of his people to save them and we will be punished for abandoning them.) **But turmoil to the inhabitants of Babylon. ³⁵"A sword against the Chaldeans," declares the LORD, "And against the inhabitants of Babylon, And against her officials and her wise men! ³⁶ "A sword against the oracle priests,** (This has reference to the churches that became part of this last pope's movement to bring all religions together.) … **and they will become fools! A sword against her mighty men, and they will be shattered!** (When the rapture is delayed.) **³⁷ "A sword against their horses and against their chariots, and against all the foreigners who are in the midst of her, and they will become women!** (This is when you will see men displayed as weak vessels.) **A sword against her treasures, and they will be plundered! ³⁸ "A drought on her waters, and they will be dried up! For it is a land of idols, and they are mad over fearsome idols. ³⁹ "Therefore the desert creatures will live there along with the jackals; The ostriches also will live in it, and it will never again be inhabited or dwelt in from generation to generation.** This is described in the seventeenth and eighteenth chapters of the book of Revelation.) **⁴⁰ "As when God overthrew Sodom and Gomorrah with its neighbors," declares the LORD, "No man will live there, nor will any son of man reside in it.** (This curse is upon our land for legalizing sodomy.) **⁴¹ "Behold, a people is coming from the north, and a great nation and many kings Will be aroused from the remote parts of the earth. ⁴² "They seize their bow and javelin; They are cruel and have no mercy.** (This is Russia and China and all our allies that joined with them when we abandoned them coming to take their Garden of Eden.) **Their voice roars like the sea, and they ride on horses, Marshalled like a man for the battle Against you, O daughter of Babylon. ⁴³ "The king of Babylon has heard the report about them, and his hands hang limp; Distress has gripped him, Agony like a woman in childbirth.** (When our leaders see our doom coming, they will begin to whale in agony in anticipation of our destruction. (Rev. 18) **⁴⁴ " Behold, one will come up like a lion from the thicket of the Jordan to a perennially watered pasture; for in an instant I shall make them run away from it, and whoever is chosen I shall appoint over it. For who is like Me, and who will summon Me into court? And who then is the shepherd who can stand before Me?" ⁴⁵ <u>Therefore hear the plan of the LORD which He has planned against Babylon, and His</u>**

purposes which He has purposed against the land of the Chaldeans: surely they will drag them off, even the little ones of the flock; (This has reference to your young daughters taken by the invading armies.) **surely He will make their pasture desolate because of them. [46] At the shout, <u>"Babylon has been seized!"</u> the earth is shaken, and an outcry is heard among the nations. Revelation 18:18-19 (NASB77) [18] and were crying out as they saw the smoke of her burning, saying, 'What city is like the great city?' [19] "And they threw dust on their heads and were crying out, weeping and mourning, saying, 'Woe, woe, the great city, in which all who had ships at sea became rich by her wealth, for in one hour she has been laid waste!'"**

The thunder judgments are the time that will be cut short for the preservation of the Earth or else the demonic spiritual forces at war in the souls of men would destroy the Earth. God himself oversees the activity that will limit the degree of destruction they can do as restoring the Earth back to the conditions that existed in the first millennium. When all is complete during the seven years of these apocalyptic changes. This is the judgment that represents the vials or bowel in Revelation, the re-alignment of the Earth's geography.

When Jesus told John not to write what he saw in Rev. 10:4; at that time, this mystery was withheld to be revealed to the last generation. All who see they have been victims of false doctrine would lose hope and a great number will be given over to the mark of the beast by not knowing this side of God as being a luke-warm confessing Christian, rejected by God spitting them out of His mouth. AMEN

The Releasing of the Spirit of Fear

Background scripture:

> *Acts 5:8-11 "(KJV) ⁸ And Peter answered unto her, Tell me whether ye sold the land for so much? And she said, Yea, for so much. ⁹ Then Peter said unto her, How is it that ye have agreed together to tempt the Spirit of the Lord? behold, the feet of them which have buried thy husband are at the door, and shall carry thee out. ¹⁰ Then fell she down straightway at his feet, and yielded up the ghost: and the young men came in, and found her dead, and, carrying her forth, buried her by her husband. ¹¹ And <u>great fear came upon all the church,</u> and upon as many as heard these things."*

When I was given this passage of scripture as an opening, it seemed strange until the revelation came.

Recently in a previous chronicle, I also mentioned a spirit of fear has been released from the pit. The state of the people on a large scale are being controlled by a media psychology by electronically induced mind control through smart media devices as the **"prince of the power of the air"** rides the airwaves into your minds. The evidence is all around us as not being able to live without this beast that speaks, held in your right hand. This Has caused our attention span to be reduced to critical levels of tolerance that is leading to an increased in the number of road rage and mass suicide killings. Our willing ignorance tend to ignore all these bad news reports until it reaches home. We are in the third phase of the troubling of the waters leading up to the tribulation.

As confessing Christians, our level of knowledge in traditional church settings does not go into the layered revelations that are the mysteries the Holy Spirit wants to reveal to every one of us. Our limitation in knowledge is based in standards set by mans academia, limited to only what his father, (the devil) lead you to believe to ensure our destruction by keeping us ever learning but never coming to the truth of our eternal potential in Christ. Now to examine the background scriptures … the story of Ananias and his wife is another layered revelation story. When God's spirit returns in the latter rain, You will instantly be given over to Satan for destruction as a luke-warm Christian for not repenting when your state is revealed as living a lie. That's the curse of fear that come with living a lie. That's why, if he can get you to deny him through fear of men, he knows he has you under his control. What God has given man for his good, in an evil environment will be used to destroy him by not knowing who is in possession of his vessel. Only the bible truth can give you the knowledge to examine this type of fruit; whether it be of God or of the devil because of Satan' many disguises. **Matthew 12:33 (KJV) Matthew 12:33 "(KJV) [33] Either make the tree good, and his fruit good; or else make the tree corrupt, and his fruit corrupt: for the tree is known by his fruit. Matthew 7:16 (KJV) [16] Ye shall know them by their fruits"** … This is the third layer to the background scripture. What we are ignorant of why God destroyed a whole civilization by bringing waters of destruction out of the ground and the sky to end the first dispensation of man. We can't see our ignorance until we become the victim. The Earth was not covered with water as it is now; therefore, at the end of the sixth millenniums, God will release the enemy to send natural disasters as a sign, fires in and around your cities and waters to flood your towns. This sign is the mixture of fire and water, kept separated to serve its purpose as the coming signs of destruction. These signs represent the beginning and the end. **Revelation 18:6 "(KJV) [6] Reward her even as she rewarded you, and double unto her double according to her works: in the cup which she hath filled fill to her double. Jeremiah 50:32 (KJV) [32] And the most proud shall stumble and fall, and none shall raise him up: and <u>I will kindle a fire in his cities,</u> and it shall devour all round about him."** (Just when we think we have arrived at peace and safety.) **1 Thessalonians 5:3 "(KJV) [3] For when they shall say, Peace and safety; then sudden destruction cometh upon them, as travail upon a woman with child; and they shall not escape."**

When I hear the replies of those victims of natural disasters, I am some-what grieved that we still can't see the scope of these disasters as being signs of bible prophecy of diverse occurrences. These natural disasters around the country are judgements that are going to intensify to the point of generating fears we have never had to face in this country before. Satan has gone before God as he did with Job but this time, he has justified the destruction we see happening as evil men possessed with his spirit get worse and worse. Once again on the timeline of God, man has reached the point of no return as for prophecy being fulfilled.

This is the vision that is only given through the spirit of prophecy for all with ears to hear and eyes to see what **"Thus Say the lord."**

I don't like being the barer of such bad news but there's hope, you are being warned before the worst comes to set your house in order because none shall escape what's coming to try everyone living that name his name must prove your love for God in the fires of tribulation. I have said many … many times in these writings, there is no new things in God's sight; all history he set in motion is just repeated throughout times, ages and dispensations. **(Eccl.1:9)** Christ can't return until the church he set up as one body be restored as he established it in the beginning with the devil defeated under her feet.

Only tribulation can clean up this mass of confusion we have made in the name of God. He is now walking in the earth by his spirit selecting souls as he did that established his first church that will have to go through what the early apostles did and spill their blood once again for the last time to justify his death, burial, and resurrection before He can return. Many confessing Christians will be replaced at the marriage supper with the souls being replaced by some of their children and of those wounded at the hands of a sick divided church world. God will have mercy on some of your children and save them to replace you. The devil has invaded the assembly and turned it into and entertainment center. In my observation of these times, I see the same willing ignorance that was present in the days of Noah.

There were scoffers who mocked him for building a boat when it had never rained. This lasted for one hundred and twenty years before the judgment came with a drop of rain that came seven days after the door was closed to the Ark. That same spirit has returned to judge man again at the end of his time to subdue the earth. Remember, **"911"** was a distress call marked by a major sign of the fall of the twin towers in Modern Babylon … **Ezekiel 26:9" (KJV) 9 And he shall set engines** (Airplanes hitting the World Trade Towers) **of war against thy walls, and with his axes he shall break down thy towers."** The place where this sign will be given is described in … **Isaiah 30:25 "(KJV) 25 And there shall be upon every high mountain, and upon every high hill,**

rivers and streams of waters <u>in the day of the great slaughter, when the towers fall</u>." This is a description of the World Trade Towers surrounded by water on the lower end of Manhattan Island in New York. I want you to see how detailed our future history is repeated by the interpretation of the signs Jesus told us to watch in our time as revealed through the spirit of prophecy.

God has delayed our judgment day to give his elects in the wilderness time to get ready to revive his church out of great tribulation to enter his kingdom. **Acts 14:22 "(KJV) ²² Confirming the souls of the disciples, and exhorting them to continue in the faith, and that we must through much tribulation enter into the kingdom of God."**

If you want to be able to see in the spirit on this level, you must forsake your own thoughts and conclusions about what you see because the kingdom of God does not come by observation in the natural order; observations are the end result of the signs. That's why those you try to predict by observation will always get it wrong … **Luke 17:20 "(KJV) ²⁰ And when he was demanded of the Pharisees, when the kingdom of God should come, he answered them and said, The kingdom of God cometh not with observation":** One of the reasons I see pastors and so called prophets burn-out mode today is lack of vision in their messages by trying to help the Holy Spirit in their seminary trained intellect instead of releasing him to feed the assembly what they need spiritually. In their own strength, they are trying to keep their members from sleeping through the service. Jesus said … **John 12:32 "(KJV) ³² And I, if I be lifted up from the earth, will draw all men unto me."** Self-denial is where we see Jesus feeding his church the true spiritual bread that delivers the soul.

The few times I have had the privilege to give a message in an assembly, I did not see anyone sleeping. Most of them was astonished at the depth of the message. I learned in my profession death can be sudden and inevitable; it will come to us all and some without notice. I have found that dying to yourself first is how you will literally overcome the fear of dying from this life. I strive to think as though I am living in the fullness in order that he may find the faith in me he expects to see in me as trusting him, this time in my body. This mind-set has help me overcome many attacks of the devil in my body and circumstances beyond my control.

I still have faults that cause me to make mistakes and miss the mark sometimes in judgments because of the distraction I encounter in my daily walk. Thank God for grace and mercy. If you can be honest with God, you will be honest with others. Never forget that it is God you should fear, not man. Sense God open my mind to the things as in … **Jeremiah 33:3 "(KJV) ³ Call unto me, and I will answer thee, and shew thee great and mighty things, which thou knowest not"** … I have never been the same nor have many understood me to a certain degree. The reason I'm speaking in such a way is because I wish all could see beyond your fleshy existence with a deeper understanding of God's concepts of life in this world.

Not that I have arrived, I now know what Paul saw while in this state of mind and this is without literally seeing dreams or vision as some others. I have learned as to what God is doing in all things is to wait for the fruit as to the heart of the source. You may be saying, *why we don't hear of you if you are having this type of relationship with the lord as seeing people getting healed and delivered?* What I'm being taught is not to be manifested until the people are in a condition where they are ready to hear what they have ignored. God is not going to waste this word on those who have had all this time to hear his voice just to reject Him. Many with-out knowing have had their day of visitation and had they known his voice would be prepared for what's coming. When our economy collapses and all you depend on is gone, that will be the time I have been informing you to prepare for.

Although I have been brought to understand revelations beyond my level of comprehension, God is ready to have this kind of relationship with anyone that gives him your mind and quit trusting in yourself. The way to get to have this kind of unconditional love is total surrender as in … **Matthew 6:33 "(KJV) 33 But seek ye first the kingdom of God, and his righteousness; and all these things shall be added unto you."** If you are continually having trouble in your spirit, soul and body, it is a sign that you are holding on to something you need to let go. This is the healing part of the mind of God when you are loosed from the entanglements of this world that will transform and transport you into the kingdom of heaven. What grieves me is to know the persons problem and God said they are not ready to hear you; so, you must just follow peace because you are on God's timing as to when to speak. This you can do when you exercise temperance. Quite people are good listeners, that' why you are surprised at what they say when they speak. AMEN

Now on the national front

The Obama Affordable Health Care Act was written in such a way that it cannot be change; therefore, what you see the Republicans trying to do will only add a burden or take away the benefits to the people it was designed to help. This type of legislation should have been written shortly after the Social Security act; we as Americans would have perfected the health care system and contained the cost by having one of the best delivery systems as supported by withholding both taxes at that time that would have insured equal opportunity to quality healthcare. That's a Christian nation taking care of all it's citizens equally.

This bill, written at this late stage in time, has come when the system of health care is too corrupted with fraudulent means of delivery without specific oversight guideline in place for providers that have taken advantage by overbilling for services they have not provided. The "Obama Care" bill was passed fifty years too late at a cost that is far too high to sustain; once implemented, the twenty million people that benefited at that time in the first year is what the Republicans will have trouble within their attempts to make changes.

The economy cannot sustain itself with this belated added expense of the Obama bill that was crafted in such a way that does not leave any wiggle room without upsetting those that got insured when it was first implemented. This bill effected your health care by making it affordable by adding supplements from the government. Now the House and Senate are in a dilemma that is beyond party lines. They are trying to change what was done at the expense of not counting the cost at the time Obama Care was introduced.

Now we are in the third year when that cost is now realized but those on it don't want to give it up and they can't come up with a workable alternative. That's the quagmire that will cause a national crisis that they have found themselves in in the Houses of Representatives. This is very simple to correct but their party loyalty comes before our national priority. Instead of improving on what's good for all regardless of party, they used the wrong term "repeal and replace" instead of improving; here you see where the return of prejudice spirits against people of color just for getting this bill through on President Obama's watch. The Republicans, using that term "repeal" after it was put into law and implemented is where they see the problem they have created by trying to reverse Obama's legacy that reveals their hidden prejudices. The public has no idea of what the government is doing that is causing all these divisions in the two parties that is contributing to our internal collapse by inflating the real-estate market to a bubble that burst in 2008.

The banks back with a hidden agenda as being controlled by the powers that are currently controlling Washington, DC; inflated the economy to robbed the middle class of high paying jobs that contributed to high manufacturing cost as being made in America. They had to correct their financial instability. This all happen behind closed doors. In their secrete chambers, cause that 1% to get richer to the point of controlling 99% of the nation's wealth. The people that are behind this economic change in the transfer of wealth are the members of The New World Order. Donald Trump has been compromised through our number one enemy, Russia. Isn't it strange that his administration will not say anything against Russia with all the evidence we have on their hacking activity. All the spy agencies are supporting these allegations but not his administration. He called it **"fake News,"** That's because he was a conspiracy theorist believer. In the spirit of truth, a lot of news is reported along political lines. These revelations will be known soon.

Just like I never thought I would see a president of the free world endorse Sodomy and the very next one come into to this office on his own terms in the history of presidential elections. Never in our history had of this type dictate his own terns in a campaign and succeed in getting elected by his own rules. That's why he stays in touch with his supporters as still in campaign mode. The billionaires in his cabinet are the people put there to begin implementing our downfall to bring in the N.W.O. The people got what they wanted, and they have their patsy in place for their final assault on this nation. He is the Cyrus of our times biblically, as a none political leader.

This has been sixty years in the making. The Obama presidency is officially the last president that would represent any dignity in the office as President of the free world. He would be the fulfillment of Dr. M. L. Kings prophecy dream of a man of color would come in this office on the bassist of the content of his character not the color of his skin. Trump, chosen by people in a state of delusion did not command the office by popular vote but once again, a majority Republican Electoral College, voting in their favor in a close call to the point that God gave the people what they ask for, not by popular vote but by an election default. Through him we will see what patriotic pride will cost this nation in its blind state to become the victims of destruction at the hand of a foolish president. If you have been reading and studying these chronicles, you have enough visional information to read and discern these signs. Yes, he will do some good things but ultimately, he will take the fall on his watch. Pray for him that God will give us time to reach more souls. AMEN

The Third Layer of Salvation

Background scripture:

> **2 Thessalonians 2:7 "(KJV) ⁷For the mystery of iniquity doth already work: only he who now letteth will let, until he be taken out of the way."**

The depth of my writings is design to make you think about the seriousness of our salvation as to have no doubt of what God has given us and made available as we receive Christ as our savior.

Living in the reality of the new birth; I, in my earlier years as a confessing Christian, went on for more than twenty years operating in the first stage of my salvation. It was not until I was drawn in by the Holy Spirit as to my calling as a messenger, I begin to search into the total deliverance aspect that came with my salvation. I learn have why some confessing Christians will have to be allowed to suffer sickness unto death; for some, this is the only way they will continue to serve the lord. God knows you better than you know yourself and allows certain things to remain in your life to keep you save until death. Once I asked a person this question? If you were completely healed, what would you do; their reply, all the things I never could do before. That statement didn't represent a real love for God, so I ask God to do according to His will. When Jesus said, it's was according to your faith, I have never been sick with and illness that I didn't get delivered from. I learn what can justifying him remaining on you. I begin to study what being converted really means and is and what gives you authority over the devil that when Jesus said … **Matthew 18:3 "(KJV) ³And said, Verily I say unto you, except ye be converted, and become as little children, ye shall not enter into the kingdom of heaven."** Children are not born with doubt or worries; that comes from your environment. During the seven years of my re-teaching by the Holy Spirit, I wanted to know what I HAD TO DO TO NOT BE A WORRIER ABOUT ANYTHING THAT HAD DELIVERED ME FROM. **Matthew 13:15**

"(KJV) [15] For this people's heart is waxed gross, and their ears are dull of hearing, and their eyes they have closed; lest at any time they should see with their eyes, and hear with their ears, and should understand with their heart, and should be converted, and I should heal them." This scripture by lack of understanding kept me bound in a traditional church environment where this knowledge was not taught in the kind of faith to get healed and stay healed. When the Holy Spirit got my attention, I started to look at the life of Jesus as he lived and walked while on this earth for that short span of three and one-half years he demonstrated what the father would do in them that followed his example.

I had been taught that we couldn't be as holy as Jesus. In the first stage of salvation, this makes sense because we are baby Christians when we first encounter truth. Now there is the second layer to study and learn why I'm called a new creature and what do we have that we didn't have before. This is all up to you to seek out the answer to these questions and ask God to increase your faith to believe what he is telling you through his word. **Matthew 6:33 "(KJV) [33] But seek ye first the kingdom of God, and his righteousness; and all these things shall be added unto you."** In that love he has given us, we must maintain that will gives us the ability to look beyond the faults of others with this mindset … **1 Corinthians 2:2 "(KJV) [2] For I determined not to know any thing among you, save Jesus Christ, and him crucified."** When you realize that we all came from sin to salvation, that's why you can't judge another with-out condemning yourself. Instead of judging, you are to become what they are not by letting the Holy Spirit lift Jesus. The key is to surrender with a child-like faith.

This I found out was the reason for my short comings that seem to ware me out by asking God to forgive me many times for things I should have overcome by knowledge. After a while I soon learned it was my environment that was causing my problem. I was trying to do this in my own strength by not surrendering fully when you are around people that are continuing to sin; you will also. Now this was the hard part that we have all had trouble with if you are honest with yourself … **Ephesians 5:11 "(KJV) [11] And have no fellowship with the unfruitful works of darkness, but rather reprove them. 2 Corinthians 6:17 (KJV) [17] Wherefore come out from among them, and be ye separate, saith the Lord, and touch not the unclean thing; and I will receive you, John 15:18 (KJV) [18] If the world hate you, ye know that it hated me before it hated you. John 7:7 (KJV) [7] The world cannot hate you; but me it hateth, because I testify of it, that the works thereof are evil. Amos 3:3 (KJV) [3] Can two walk together, except they be agreed?"** If you continue to keep company with a person that is sinning … **2 John 1:11 "(KJV) [11] For he that biddeth him God speed is partaker of his evil deeds."** God considers you as condoning the works of the devil. The only way that person will know whether you believe what you confess to be is by not keeping company with them in their sinful state. **1 Thessalonians 4:7 "(KJV) [7] For God hath not called us unto uncleanness, but unto holiness."**

Fact one. You do not have anything to offer God that he did not give you; that is, your life. Our wickedness is what convicted us when we saw it presented to us by the Holy Spirit. Therefore … **Isaiah 55:7-8 "(KJV) [7] Let the wicked forsake his way,** (we were born that way) **and the unrighteous man his thoughts:** (This is where your conviction causes you to surrender because you will see you are a victim of your own thinking.) **and let him return unto the LORD, and he will have mercy upon him; and to our God, for he will abundantly pardon.** (This is what he does as the first stage to becoming a new creature?) **[8] For my thoughts are not your thoughts, neither are your ways my ways, saith the LORD."** (As you see, this was required in the old covenant to follow the commandments of God to be accepted. Now this is where the sacrifice of yourself will transform the whole man back to that new creature and take him out of the natural temple as Christ enters you as his new temple dwelling place now as walking by faith … **1 John 4:4 (KJV) [4] Ye are of God, little children, and have overcome them: because greater is he that is in you, than he that is in the world. 1 Corinthians 6:19 "(KJV) [19] What? know ye not that your body is the temple of the Holy Ghost which is in you, which ye have of God, and ye are not your own? Romans 12:1-2 (KJV) [1] I beseech you therefore, brethren, by the mercies of God, that ye present your bodies a living sacrifice, holy, acceptable unto God, which is your reasonable service. [2] And be not conformed to this world: but be ye transformed by the renewing of your mind, that ye may prove what is that good, and acceptable, and perfect, will of God."** The law did not make men sin free because he remained natural and had to use an animal's blood to atone for his sins in the old covenant. Jesus gave up his will, sacrificed his life-giving blood so the father could receive all men created in his image. Therefore, Jesus is our only example to us in our body that this can be done but only in the same way Jesus did; surrender you will. This is what you will have to learn and act upon in his word as the beginning stages to walk as a new creature. This stage two.

Fact two: It took faith to get saved, now you must … **Hebrews 11:6 "(KJV) [6] But without faith it is impossible to please him: for he that cometh to God must believe that he is, and that he is a rewarder of them that diligently seek him."** The faith that God has made available to them that name his name is found in the whole council of the truth applied in all arrears of your life. The whole man walks the privilege of the new creature in the authority as the Adam restored. This is where we will begin to demonstrate the pure Agape love of God in Christ to the world that can only be seen in his purity by a dying vessel being made meat for the master's consumption. This is what will bring separations from the world as he receives you into the family of God. You are now walking on that … **Matthew 7:14 "(KJV) ¹⁴ Because strait is the gate, and narrow is the way, which leadeth unto life, and few there be that find it."** All my short-comings can be measured in unlearning the hear-say teachings through man that meant well but lacked revelation knowledge by not paying the price for the lord to show up in the assembly as he did in the early church established through the apostles. All who refuse to except God's invitation … **John 8:24 "(KJV) ²⁴ I   said therefore unto you, that ye shall die in your sins: for if ye believe not that I am he, ye shall die in your sins."** If you fail to continue in him, you will die spiritually by committing the sins of omission. Dying to self is what brings you to this this third layer of complete deliverance.

The third and final layer of complete deliverance.

This is where you overcome the fear of death and dying. We don't' like to think of literally dying but the reality is, it's the destiny of us all. We are born a child whose destiny is hell if we never claim our birth-rite to live for eternity when called by the Holy Spirit the day we hear the gospel. We were born under curse of the law of sin and death as a child of the devil. I, after having heard of the miracles that evangelist was seeing in third world countries is representative of how far we have fallen from the anointed presence of the Holy Spirit in our assemblies. It is hard to get people to believe in miracles when they don't see them as in the early church. The person that has unwavering faith in the full council of the word can keep the devil off him in every area of your life just by believing and acting on the word without doubt in his heart. This is the heritage that came when Jesus said, **"It is finish;"** now all we must do is stand on his word and watch him perform it according to your faith in every area of your life. **Jeremiah 1:12 "(KJV) ¹² Then said the LORD unto me, thou hast well seen: for I will hasten my word to perform it."** In my inquiry of why we don't see the miracles in the assembly like this anymore, this was my reply … **Mark 11:17 "(KJV) ¹⁷ And he taught, saying unto them, is it not written, my house shall be called of all nations the house of prayer? but ye have made it a den of thieves."**

When I was growing up in church as a young boy, I recalled every Wednesday night the people would come together and pray for an hour in the church. They called it prayer meeting night. They would anoint with oil, anyone who was sick. The women were more faithful at doing this than the men and some got delivered from sickness. I recall as a young child, the early saints were poor in spirit, but they were faithful to the lord in their prayer life.

Matthew 5:3 "(KJV) ³ Blessed are the poor in spirit: for theirs is the kingdom of heaven." I personally have been working on my own faith in this area to remove all doubt and I'm beginning to see some results in those I have taught how to deliver yourself just by standing on the word with no conditions, just putting God to the test. If you ever want to get to this third layer in your salvation, this is the faith He seeks to find when He returns. You must learn to trust in Him without doubting. That's when you are a converted new creation, Christ can lift himself up in you and draw those he has purposed to save using your vessel.

The point I want to leave you with is not to doubt your salvation because this can be a little strong for some of you; I want you to know the truth that will set you free are the benefits that came with your salvation. Now it's up to you to take back what the devil stole from you by having the faith to act and stand on his word. Even if you act on that word to remain faithful until death, you are in a win-win situation; you died standing in his word. You are going to die; why not die trusting him by standing on his word in the faith he expects to find in you that will give him the glory exercising his fruits in the spirit. This is our goal in the spirit while in this world but as he said, only a few will find it to this degree. That's why the church must go through tribulation, so the world can see the real God of Abraham, Isaac, and Jacob as the lord our God as one and once again to see ordinary men in his image do extraordinary things in the fullness. AMEN

The Gathering of Souls

Background scripture:

> Revelation 14:15-16 "(KJV) [15] And another angel came out of the temple, crying with a loud voice to him that sat on the cloud, Thrust in thy sickle, and reap: for the time is come for thee to reap; for the harvest of the earth is ripe. (1 Thessalonians 4:16-17 (KJV) [16] For the Lord himself shall descend from heaven with a shout, with the voice of the archangel, and with the trump of God: and the dead in Christ shall rise first:" 1 Corinthians 15:52 "(KJV) [52] In a moment, in the twinkling of an eye, at the last trump: for the trumpet shall sound, and the dead shall be raised incorruptible, and we shall be changed." Ezekiel 37:12 (KJV) [12] Therefore prophesy and say unto them, thus saith the Lord GOD; Behold, O my people, I will open your graves, and cause you to come up out of your graves, and bring you into the land of Israel.") *Cont.* [17] Then we which are alive *and* remain shall be caught up together with them in the clouds, to meet the Lord in the air: and so shall we ever be with the Lord. [16] And he that sat on the cloud thrust in his sickle on the earth; and the earth was reaped." Revelation 7:9 (KJV) [9] After this I beheld, and, lo, a great multitude, which no man could number, of all nations, and kindreds, and people, and tongues, stood before the throne, and before the Lamb, clothed with white robes, and palms in their hands;"

This mystery of the gathering of souls from Adam to those that die in the lord unto this very day are now in the third heaven being judged by Christ and the twenty-four elders. This is the destiny of all the saints that died after the first resurrection that took them out of paradise to the third heaven where Paul was when he was stoned. The second resurrection or rapture will be the last gathering as explained in above scriptures that will restore the glory of the former rain with a latter one before the closing of the doors of all that will be saved at the end of the sixth millennium.

What I have been made to see is what will determine your status in the judgment. This was for my benefit in answer to one of my inquiries of the judgment of the saints that I can now reveal to those with ears to hear. Just as I mentioned in the last update **"The Third layer of Salvation,"** Christ died to make you a completely restored version of Adam. When you fall in love with him to the point of total surrender. At that time, you will be walking in heavenly places in Christ Jesus. Sin separated Adams's present from God. That's why Adam hid from God in the garden. We who are born in sin as a result will hide from God too until he calls you unto himself. Until that time, you hid from the gospel as being a child of the devil. Your fears came from the devil; that's why Adam hid in fear when he heard the voice of God. **John 6:44 "(KJV) 44 No man can come to me, except the Father which hath sent me draw him: and I will raise him up at the last day."** You will never in your flesh state comprehend the reality of your sins and their consequences until God revealed them through his word. **John 6:40 "(KJV) 40 And this is the will of him that sent me, that everyone which seeth the Son, and believeth on him, may have everlasting life: and I will raise him up at the last day."** This is the work of the Holy Spirit sent to gather souls for the kingdom of God. If you ever deny your salvation by your actions and in words by continuing in sin and die in that state, the law of sins and death will claim you for hell. **(Gal.5:19-21)** They will send you to the Great White Throne Judgment seat of the wicked dead. I was given a greater understanding of these two scriptures … **Matthew 19:30 "(KJV) 30 But many that are first shall be last; and the last shall be first. Matthew 20:16 (KJV) 16 So the last shall be first, and the first last: for many are called, but few chosen."** This is what I saw through the spirit of God … not many well-known men who was given this privilege to build God's kingdom endured when the blessings came and over-took them for the glory of men and in the sight of God, they became the least.

This I know because I was convicted under these doctrines of men and remain in error for thirty years. Many of them sought God for what he gave them without counting the cost of temptations when the blessings overtook them by claiming God's heritage for themselves. This is why … **1 Corinthians 1:26 "(KJV) 26 For ye see your calling, brethren, how that not many wise men after the flesh, not many mighty, not many noble, are called:"** Matthew 19:24 **"(KJV) 24 And again I say unto you, It is easier for a camel to go through the eye of a needle, than for a rich man to enter into the kingdom of God."**

This is the temptation that has befallen many of them; they exchange the glory of God for the glory of men. Only those that repented when God revealed the state of their heart are received in heaven before they died; there, they will become the least and the last in the judgment for taking God's glory. Outside of the four and twenty elders, many of the thrones of glory are still empty and reserved for those who endure the testimony of Jesus Christ in tribulation where many will not speak well of you that walk Godly on this earth. **2 Timothy 3:12 "(KJV) ¹² Yea, and all that will live godly in Christ Jesus shall suffer persecution." Luke 6:26 (KJV) ²⁶ Woe unto you, when all men shall speak well of you! for so did their fathers to the false prophets."** I am not saying that I have reach that stage of Godly living in the fullness but in striving to arrive, there have been many separations and outright rejections when you choose to go the way of the cross to obtain that crown of glory.

It was revealed to me that many women will sit on those thrones. This is where I learned that men of renowned status will react like the Pharisees to them that carry this unadulterated truth when they don't want to be rebuked by God because they are in love with the glory of men and the blessings of this world. Many have closed their doors to the prophet's vision and when God sends the least of men to warn them, many souls will perish under them that refuse to leave. **Proverbs29:18 (KJV) ¹⁸ Where there is no vision, the people perish: but he that keepeth the law, happy is he.**

All those with ears to hear will receive that word and become as the wise virgins with gladness at their day of redemption. This is the pride that God hates that many spiritual leaders are infected with in these last days. When God extends his grace to call them to repent, many will become the least in heaven for their efforts in trying to help him; had they not repented when God gave them another chance, they would have come up in the Great White Throne Judgment. **Jude 1:11 "(KJV) ¹¹ Woe unto them! for they have gone in the way of Cain and ran greedily after the error of Balaam for reward and perished in the gainsaying of Core."** Having faith is what got us saved but using it to gain all the goods of this world will cause you to lose your love of God in the Holy Spirit that produce fruit that remain. The fullness of his glory is available to all men but only a few as elects will receive it. **Matthew 16:26 "(KJV) ²⁶ For what is a man profited, if he shall gain the whole world, and lose his own soul? or what shall a man give in exchange for his soul?"** The few that are given a throne room experience will carry the mantle of Jesus in humility. A great many of people in heaven that will occupy these thrones will not be well known in this world, yet this is where they earned that privileged by not taking God's glory as they were being used in their calling. They suffered along with Christ; this time in their bodies to get the reward. This is where I saw that many faithful women in this area that remained obedient in their place as God used them. They resisted the temptation to usurp authority over the male image as jezebels. They are the prayer warriors that keep God's house in order. I have read some of the testimonies of men who said they visited with Christ in heaven. They think that that experience gave them favor with God with-out knowing, this can be a point of your deception when you think of yourself more highly than you should by having that experience. That's why I quick thinking so I can see who is of God.

Those on those thrones, died to their flesh to show God how much they loved Him by letting Jesus be seen and not them. These are in the numberless multitude of saints that are looking down on this last generation to see the glory that they did not get to see because of their error in ministering while on Earth. God had given them a pure love that would have caused many more souls to be brought in with fruit that remained under their ministries had they not been tempted to compromise or take the glory of men.

Their status is that of the foolish virgins that lost their oil and only redeemed enough to obtain grace to be saved from the error of their ways. Those who sowed discord that caused divisions among the body are the ones that brought diseases upon themselves and to their assemblies that drank the cup of bitterness that Satan justified before God to take them down. **Isaiah 9:16 "(KJV) ¹⁶ For the leaders of this people cause them to err;** (Many of God's innocent souls were led into the hands of the devil by the error of their ways and teachings that caused them to be destroyed before their time.) **And they that are led of them are destroyed." Isaiah 3:12 (KJV) ¹² As for my people, children are their oppressors, and women rule over them. O my people, they which lead thee cause thee to err, and destroy the way of thy paths."**

God allowed Satan to take them out by letting a disease come upon them to destroy them for not repenting in their day of visitation; those that do will receive grace but will be the least in heaven. Never appoint yourself an authority on what God is doing while ministering in your flesh. No man on earth has all the answers in the word but only the Holy Ghost. He only lift Jesus not flesh because we did not come from heaven. That's why God gave the gifts in a diverse manner to make us interdependent on each other as a body united in Him. If you allow Satan to set yourself up as a spokesman in the flesh for God when he can speak for himself, you have taken the place of the Holy Spirit in your flesh and will be confounded in the end when this happens to you.

Satan will give you a false sense of humility. All who remain humble will see Christ as their head and remain that way until death. **Isaiah 50:7 "(KJV) ⁷ For the Lord GOD will help me; therefore, shall I not be confounded: therefore,** have I set my face like a flint, and I know that I shall not be ashamed. **Psalm 25:20 (KJV) 20 O keep my soul and deliver me: let me not be ashamed; for I put my trust in thee."** We are in no position to judge another sense none of came from heaven. Only those God chose to manifest himself in will let him speak and demonstrate this love that looks beyond our faults to show us what we need that only he can give. None of us can hide from truth when we are exposed. Sense my encounter with the truth as taught by the Holy Spirit, I am thoroughly convinced that I'm but dust in the image of my creator to be used by God and if I remain in the background for him to get the glory he so richly deserves for this privilege, I get the reward to be with him for eternity. Now that's saving yourself!

"Love your enemies" as a new creature, representing good. You are looking at your old self in them before God called you out to now be a light to them that are now without. There's no little sin. **1 John 5:17 "(KJV) 17 All unrighteousness is sin: and there is a sin not unto death."**

The way God taught me to win the favor of my extended family is by actions more than words. I had to learn when to act and when to speak. I learn to let my actions follow my words. Don't beat yourself up when you make a mistake or even fail; if they are not forgiving, this is how you find out who really has God's love in them. Many of those that followed Jesus were not there for the word but for what they could get that only he had to give. When he allowed himself to be humiliated on the cross, those with pride turned away and they will do the same to you when you become as humble as Christ; then you will experience what real strength is because he will be the only one there with you in the end. Remember, it is the least among men that will let the glory of God be seen and they will be the ones to sit on those thrones if you eat his flesh and drink his blood all the way to your cross.

This is how Jesus replied to the women that ask to let her son sit with him on his throne … **Matthew 20:20-23 "(JKV)20 Then came to him the mother of Zebedee's children with her sons, worshipping him, and desiring a certain thing of him. 21 And he said unto her, what wilt thou? She saith unto him, Grant that these my two sons may sit, the one on thy right hand, and the other on the left, in thy kingdom. 22 But Jesus answered and said, Ye know not what ye ask. Are ye able to drink of the cup that I shall drink of, and to be baptized with the baptism that I am baptized with? They say unto him, we are able. 23 And he saith unto them, Ye shall drink indeed of my cup, and be baptized with the baptism that I am baptized with: but to sit on my right hand, and on my left, is not mine to give, but it shall be given to them for**

whom it is prepared of my Father." When he revealed to me about those who are in heaven that were great men here, it was not through by open vision but by a revelation in my mind. These things the devil wouldn't reveal to you as his child. The error that caused them to become the least there, he also was giving me a choice to be one to sit on one of those thrones and what it would cost me that only he could give me the grace to endure. **"Maranatha"**

How Satan Deceived the Church World

Background Scriptures:

> *Jeremiah 14:14 "(KJV) ¹⁴ Then the LORD said unto me, the prophets prophesy lies in my name: I sent them not, neither have I commanded them, neither spake unto them: they prophesy unto you a false vision and divination, and a thing of nought, and the deceit of their heart. 1 Kings 22:22-23 (KJV) ²² And the LORD said unto him, Wherewith? And he said, I will go forth, <u>and I will be a lying spirit in the mouth of all his prophets</u>. And he said, thou shalt persuade him, and prevail also: go forth, and do so. ²³ Now therefore, behold, the LORD hath put a <u>lying spirit in the mouth of all these thy prophets</u>, and the LORD hath spoken evil concerning thee. Jeremiah 16:19 (KJV) ¹⁹ O LORD, my strength, and my fortress, and my refuge in the day of affliction, the Gentiles shall come unto thee from the ends of the earth, and shall say, <u>surely our fathers have inherited lies, vanity, and things wherein there is no profit.</u> Revelation 12:9 (KJV) ⁹ And the great dragon was cast out, that old serpent, called the Devil, and Satan, which <u>deceiveth the whole world</u>: he was cast out <u>into the earth</u>, and his angels were cast out with him. Daniel 7:25 (KJV) ²⁵ And he shall speak great words against the most High, and shall wear out the saints of the most High, and think to change times and laws: and they shall be given into his hand until a time and times and the dividing of time."*

The world's fate is already determined as the children of the Devil; however, the focus in this chronicle will be on what the church has failed to see as how it has been seduced to what is has become today. Recently, I was doing a study on the order of the Jesuits Priesthood and the influence it has on the Christian church. I was fascinated about their history as the military company of the Pope. What caught my attention is to see how this organization with tentacles' all over the world, can carry out such a mission. I will attempt to share with you what I found in this revelation of how Satan has anointed them to carry out their master plan that is manifested in the above topic and supporting scriptures.

The Jesuits are the ruling order of the Catholic Church. Its members start as Cardinals before they can qualify as a Jesuits. Their founder is St. Ignatius of Loyola. Their objective after the fall of Rome became the religious form that would be the military company to their Pope as a government that seeks to control and influence on world Governments and religions including Christianity.

They are an independent power as a self-governing religious body; as a separate state, the Vatican has achieved international immunity as a sovereign state with-in the nations they occupy. Rome was never conquered but fell from within as victims of their own greed, corruption, immorality and over taxation. Having inherited the wealth of the plunders of the knights Templar's, they emerged as a separate state operating under a religious charter. They are a highly disciplined organization with absolute devotion to their Pope. They have a ruling general that answers only to the pope. Each ruling general, hold the highest rank in the order, some are selected to be the pope. Their origin and power dates back to early Rome which confiscated the wealth plundered by the Knights Templars of the nations they raided and stored in a secret place where to this day is not known to the world. They have incorporated the knowledge from many nations cultural treasures they plundered.

Because of their vast wealth and resources, they are able to establish and support their mission around the world, build institutions of higher learning make investments in the nations they occupy to promote their agenda of world domination of religions. The process by which to become a coadjutor, culminates in the ordination as a Cardinal. This path to become a Jesuit priest takes fifteen years. At that time, he takes a vow to the pope to become a Jesuit priest of the highest order as a member of the general council to the order answerable only to the pope.

Their constitution governing their body is secret, known only to the Jesuit's; however, the central focus of their doctrine is that **"The ends justify the means end."** The absolute vow of discipline requires their members to obey their superiors even when it involves grievous sins committed among a member of the order of Jesuits. This hidden power behind the papacy that is ushering in a new Revived Roman Empire. Keep this in mind and in the above scriptures you will see how this anointing on them by Satan has brought down the church world. Through a systematic replacing of the apostle's doctrine, published and introduced new bible versions. This method of mind control by seducing spirits employs all the resources of this world at their disposal that when seduced, is so subtle, you will not even know it unless God reveals it to you. Remember, this sprit would deceive the elects if it were not for the presents of the unction anointing. As a form of a false religion, who worship in their cathedral like assembly are putting their pope up as Jesus in the flesh. That's blasphemy in God's sight. Those who worship under their doctrine has blasphemed God by giving man the power to forgive men of their sins. **Matthew 23:9 "(KJV) ⁹ And call no *man* your father upon the earth: for one is your Father, which is in heaven."** This is by observation in comparison to the doctrine of the apostles given them by Christ.

In keeping with my charge as an instrument of the Lord to reveal these end time revelations to those that have ears to hear, through this inspiration of the Holy Spirit, I can now see him filling in the hidden mysteries behind the scriptural context of the knowledge to those that have been given ears to hear. I know these chronicles may provoke some of you who may be puffed up in your own knowledge. I challenge you to search the scriptures for yourself and try the spirit of truth, but I must warn you to surrender your will first or you will be further deceived in your own thinking.

These are lying spirits they received that empowered their agenda

1. We will penetrate and establish institutions of higher learning to seduce them into our doctrine of self-empowerment through principles bible teachings in our seminaries. We must print many unauthorized versions of the bible to cause doubt and confusion. **Revelation 22:18 (KJV) "¹⁸ For I testify unto every man that heareth the words of the prophecy of this book, if any man shall add unto these things, God shall add unto him the plagues that are written in this book:"**

2. We must distort the truth to cause doubt so when they hear truth, they will not receive it. **Hosea 4:6 (KJV) "⁶ My people are destroyed for lack of knowledge: because thou hast rejected knowledge, I will also reject thee, that thou shalt be no priest to me: seeing thou hast forgotten the law of thy God, I will also forget thy children."**

3. We must keep them from being born again from above so they will continue to fear man by not knowing God. **1 John 4:18 (KJV) "¹⁸ There**

is no fear in love; but perfect love casteth out fear: because fear hath torment. He that feareth is not made perfect in love.

4. Our false prophets will demonstrate lying signs and wonders to further deceive the people by using his name. **Matthew 24:24 (KJV) "24 For there shall arise false Christs, and false prophets, and shall shew great signs and wonders; insomuch that, if it were possible, they shall deceive the very elect."**

5. We must teach them the principals of faith on a carnal level to deceive them to think that they are spiritual by enabling them to prosper in their own way. **Proverb 16:25 "There is a way that seemeth right unto a man, but the end thereof are the ways of death."**

6. We must cause them to pray in doubt so the circumstances that require patience will defeat them. **1 Timothy 2:8 (KJV) "8 I will therefore that men pray everywhere, lifting up holy hands, without wrath and doubting.**

7. We must convince them that they can never be perfect; by this they will deny God's ability to be perfect in them. **Romans 8:1 (KJV) "1 There is therefore now no condemnation to them which are in Christ Jesus, who walk not after the flesh, but after the Spirit. Matthew 5:48 (KJV) 48 Be ye therefore perfect, even as your Father which is in heaven is perfect."**

8. We must keep them in the carnal realm to be control them by the circumstances of life that keep them unstable by lack of peace. **John 14:27 (KJV) "27 Peace I leave with you, my peace I give unto you: not as the world giveth, give I unto you. Let not your heart be troubled, neither let it be afraid. Isaiah 26:3 (KJV) "3 Thou wilt keep him in perfect peace, whose mind is stayed on thee: because he trusteth in thee."**

9. We must empower their thought process to draw their own conclusions about what the bible say. **Isaiah 55:7-8 (KJV) "7 Let the wicked forsake his way, and the unrighteous man his thoughts: and let him return unto the LORD, and he will have mercy upon him; and to our God, for he will abundantly pardon. 8 For my thoughts are not your thoughts, neither are your ways my ways, saith the LORD."**

10. We must deceive them to think that they are operating under grace but in reality, their assemblies will operate under the law to keep them in

bondage not knowing that they are the temple of God. **2 Corinthians 6:16 (KJV) "¹⁶ And what agreement hath the temple of God with idols? for ye are the temple of the living God; as God hath said, I will dwell in them, and walk in them; and I will be their God, and they shall be my people."**

11. We must teach them to see their pastors in the flesh as their holy fathers to reverence them and not God. **Matthew 23:9 (KJV) "⁹ And call no man your father upon the earth: for one is your Father, which is in heaven."**

12. We must teach them to pervert the gospel by causing the world and the church to mix. **1 John 2:15 (KJV) "¹⁵ Love not the world, neither the things that are in the world. If any man love the world, the love of the Father is not in him."**

13. We must teach them to preach messages that do not deliver to fill their assemblies. **2 Timothy 3:5 (KJV) "⁵ Having a form of godliness but denying the power thereof: from such turn away."**

14. We must use secular entertainment to turn their assemblies into enter-tainment centers. **1 Timothy 4:1 (KJV) ¹ Now the Spirit speaketh expressly, that in the latter times some shall depart from the faith, giving heed to seducing spirits, and doctrines of devils.**

15. We must seduce the church with secular teachings to break down family values to empower women to under-mind the priesthood of man and destroy marriages so their children will rise up against their parents. **Isaiah 3:12 (KJV) "¹² As for my people, children are their oppressors, and women rule over them. O my people, <u>they which lead thee cause thee to err, and destroy the way of thy paths."</u>**

16. We must teach the to have a false sense of security by their love of idol possessions. **Exodus 20:3 (KJV) ³ Thou shalt have no other gods before me. 1 John 2:15 (KJV) ¹⁵ Love not the world, neither the things *that are* in the world. If any man love the world, the love of the Father is not in him.**

17. We must seduce churches to become entertainment centers that promote the preeminence of self worship. **Luke 6:26 (KJV) "²⁶ Woe unto you, when all men shall speak well of you! for so did their fathers to the false prophets."**

18. We must give them a spirit to build their individual kingdoms, therefore bringing about division among their established assemblies to promote separate new doctrines. **Ephesians 4:5 "(KJV) ⁵ One Lord, one faith, one baptism, Luke 11:17 (KJV) ¹⁷ But he, knowing their thoughts, said unto them, every kingdom divided against itself is brought to desolation; and a house divided against a house falleth."**

19. Our seminaries will teach them the art of begging to further their own agendas as hirelings. **Philippians 4:19 (KJV) "¹⁹ But my God shall supply all your need according to his riches in glory by Christ Jesus."**

20. We must keep them divided against each other so they will become offended and confused by the real truth. **Matthew 24:10 (KJV) "¹⁰ And then shall many be offended, and shall betray one another, and shall hate one another."**

21. We must entice them to judge each other by not knowing what spirit they are of. **Matthew 7:1-3 (KJV) "¹ Judge not, that ye be not judged.² For with what judgment ye judge, ye shall be judged: and with what measure ye mete, it shall be measured to you again. ³ And why beholdest thou the mote that is in thy brother's eye, but considerest not the beam that is in thine own eye?"**

22. We must blind their leaders with false teachings so they will never know the truth. **John 12:40 (KJV) "⁴⁰ He hath blinded their eyes, and hardened their heart; that they should not see with their eyes, nor understand with their heart, and be converted, and I should heal them. John 8:32 (KJV) ³² And ye shall know the truth, and the truth shall make you free."**

23. We must empower women to seduce their men and rule over them by changing the order in their assemblies. **1 Corinthians 11:3 (KJV) "³ But I would have you know, that the head of every man is Christ; and the head of the woman is the man; and the head of Christ is God. 1 Timothy 2:12 (KJV) ¹² But I suffer not a woman to teach, nor to usurp authority over the man, but to be in silence. Titus 2:4 (KJV) ⁴ That they may teach the young women to be sober, to love their husbands, to love their children,"**

24. We will infiltrate their seminaries to change their doctrines to mix with the world. **1 Timothy 6:3-4 (KJV) "³ If any man teach otherwise, and consent not to wholesome words, even the words of our Lord Jesus**

Christ, and to the doctrine which is according to godliness; ⁴ He is proud, knowing nothing, but doting about questions and strifes of words, whereof cometh envy, strife, railings, evil surmisings, 2 Corinthians 6:17 (KJV) ¹⁷ Wherefore come out from among them, and be ye separate, saith the Lord, and touch not the unclean thing; and I will receive you,"

25. We must gradually infiltrate our doctrine into their assemblies. Their pastors must become an idol to lord over them from the pulpit. **Psalm 146:3 (KJV) "³ Put not your trust in princes, nor in the son of man, in whom there is no help."**

26. We must deceive them with religious spirits and keep them in sin and think they are acceptable to God. **Proverbs 14:12 (KJV) ¹² There is a way which seemeth right unto a man, but the end thereof are the ways of death."**

27. We must convince them not to believe in New Testament prophets so they will not receive the warnings of their times. **Amos 3:7 (KJV) Surely the Lord GOD will dnothing, but he revealeth his secret unto his servants the prophets. Ephesians 3:5 (KJV) ⁵ Which in other ages was not made known unto the sons of men, as it is now revealed unto his holy apostles and prophets by the Spirit;"**

28. We must transform their religions into ritual, programs and traditions of man; teach them bible principles to deceived them into thinking they are saved. **Mark 7:9 (KJV) "⁹ And he said unto them, Full well ye reject the commandment of God, that ye may keep your own tradition. Hosea 4:6 (KJV) ⁶ My people are destroyed for lack of knowledge: because thou hast rejected knowledge, I will also reject thee, that thou shalt be no priest to me: seeing thou hast forgotten the law of thy God, I will also forget thy children."**

29. We will set up nonprofit corporations that will cause them to be subject to the state. **(501-C-3)** (The Catholic Church operates under 501-C-8 as a separate state). **Acts 5:29 (KJV) ²⁹ "Then Peter and the other apostles answered and said, we ought to obey God rather than men.**

30. We must produce renowned authoritative heads of these Christian corporations to promote their secular material so the people will not read their bible. **Exodus 19:5 (KJV) "⁵ Now therefore, if ye will obey my voice indeed, and keep my covenant, then ye shall be a peculiar**

treasure unto me above all people: for all the earth is mine: 2 Timothy 2:15 (KJV) [15] Study to shew thyself approved unto God, a workman that needeth not to be ashamed, rightly dividing the word of truth."

31. We must seduce them into immorality to replace the midwifes with male doctors to discover their secret parts and defile their women causing them to abort children God gave them. **Exodus 1:19-21 (KJV) "[19] And the midwives said unto Pharaoh, Because the Hebrew women are not as the Egyptian women; for they are lively, and are delivered ere the midwives come in unto them. [20] Therefore <u>God dealt well with the midwives:</u> and the people multiplied, and waxed very mighty. [21] And it came to pass, because the midwives feared God, that he made them houses. Isaiah 3:17 (ASV) [17] therefore the Lord will smite with a scab the crown of the head of the daughters of Zion, and Jehovah will lay bare their <u>secret parts.</u>"** (Men delivering babies) **Ezekiel 16:36 (KJV) [36] Thus saith the Lord GOD; Because thy filthiness was poured out, and thy <u>nakedness discovered</u> through thy whoredoms with thy lovers, and with all the idols of thy abominations, and by the blood of thy children,** (Abortions) **which thou didst give unto them;"**

32. We must create an immoral environment in their assemblies with the introduction of secular music to promote sensuality, fornication and adultery. **2 Timothy 3:6 (KJV) "[6] For of this sort are they which creep in houses, and lead captive silly women laden with sins, led away with divers lusts,"**

33. In the end we will succeed in bringing all religions under one world rule. **Revelation 12:9 (NASB77) [9] And the great dragon was thrown down, the serpent of old who is called the devil and Satan, who deceives the whole world; he was thrown down to the earth, and his angels were thrown down with him.**

My beloved brothers and sisters, these are the (33) agendas God has allowed Satan to use to deceived religious men and defiled the Church of Christ, seduced many assemblies to fulfill the great apostasy of this end time. The Jesuit order succeeded in their institutions of higher learning to reduce the church to where we are today; victims of logical theology. Now to link them to all these agendas, let's go back to the opening background scriptures. God uses these principalities under satanic influence to carry out the word spoken by the prophets that all may be fulfilled in the timeline of man. **1 Kings 22:22-23 "(KJV) "²²And the LORD said unto him, Wherewith? And he said, I will go forth, and <u>I will be a lying spirit in the mouth of all his prophets.</u>"** God set the course of events in his sovereign will from the beginning of time; now sin is just running its course, knowing the end from the beginning. **(Isa.46:10)**

These will be the false prophets that will bring the lies to seduce the church. **And he said, thou shalt persuade him, and prevail also: go forth, and do so. ²³ Now therefore, behold, <u>the LORD hath put a lying spirit in the mouth of all these thy prophets, and the LORD hath spoken evil concerning thee.</u>"** This is where you see the sovereignty of God at work controlling all things. **Jeremiah 14:14 (KJV) "¹⁴Then the LORD said unto me, the prophets prophesy lies <u>in my name</u>: I sent them not, neither have I commanded them, neither spake unto them: they prophesy unto you a false vision and divination, and a thing of nought, and the deceit of their heart. 2 Thessalonians 2:9 (KJV) ⁹Even him, whose coming is after the working of Satan with all power and signs and lying wonders, Jeremiah 16:19 (KJV) ¹⁹O LORD, my strength, and my fortress, and my refuge <u>in the day of affliction</u>, the Gentiles shall come unto thee from the ends of the earth, and shall say, <u>surely our fathers</u>** … the pastors that were seduced to believe these lies and led their congregations into idol worship. **<u>have inherited lies, vanity, and things wherein there is no profit</u>.** This declaration describes the state of the Church when the prophet brings the message of the last day. Satan has been allowed to deceive the whole world. **Revelation 12:9 (KJV) "⁹And the great dragon was cast out, that old serpent, called the Devil, and Satan, which <u>deceiveth the whole world</u>:"**

He did this while performing God's sovereign will so none would escape the judgment. **He was cast out into the earth, and his angels were cast out with him.** The fall of man invoked God's plan of redemption while in the presents of these fallen beings in the form of demonic seducing spirits. **Revelation 16:14 (KJV) "¹⁴For they are the spirits of devils, working miracles, which go forth unto the kings of the earth and of the whole world, to gather them to the battle of that great day of God Almighty.** Now you see how God allowed the Jesuit order to spread lies that would change the order of service to a form that denies the deity of Christ. This one organization alone will be responsible for the rise of the false prophet in the form of a new world religion. **<u>The ends justify the means</u>** of which they, under the inspiration of Satan's false vision are the architects of this New World Religion, the revived Roman Empire. Our pastors now are Popes in the pulpits.

These are some observations of the doctrine perpetrated by the Jesuit's?

1. 1. They do not ordain women as priest. We so called Christians ordain Women as pastors. There is no scriptural justification for this type of ordination.

2. 2. They do not promote abortions. Today, some churches now condoned this practice.

3. 3. Although recent revelations exposed the immorality with-in their order, it is not an open admission in the papacy. Today the church openly condones homosexuality even to the point of ordaining gay pastors and bishops. This is their influence manifested in the church today; the Pope is worshiped as the Holy Father; Christians worship the pastors as their holy fathers. This is the form of godliness we have been reduced too. This is noted by the **renowned** status we have elevated pastors today. The pastors pilfer the people to further their own kingdom building agendas; **the ends justifies the means to build their kingdoms**. The tithe system under the law will be the means to justify the building of their separate kingdoms.

This is a Jesuit teaching that furthers their agendas. The principals are in agreement. **Last,** whether the Church believes it or not, the Jesuits have studied the prophets; God gave them a lying spirit to make them think they can change history and the course of events. They have been instrumental in fulfilling **(Dan. 7:25)** Today, the Church do not believe in prophet as in the Old Testament, the manifestation of this false teaching that rejects them is the doctrine of rapture and prosperity. They think they are going to fly out of here before trouble starts.

My fellow brothers and sisters, it has been my assignment as one of the messengers of God to reveal some of the mysteries, kept to be revealed to those that have ears to hear and eyes to see who are at rest. It is to open our minds to the deeper things of God, as we are seeking him in this hour for the fullness of his manifestation. I hope to hear your testimonies in heaven of how we got over by the blood of the lamb and the grace of God's mercy. AMEN.

The Beast and the False Prophet

Background scripture:

> Revelation 16:13 "(KJV) [13] And I saw three unclean spirits like frogs *come* out of the mouth of the dragon, and out of the mouth of the beast, and out of the mouth of the false prophet. Revelation 19:20 (KJV) [20] And the beast was taken, and with him the false prophet that wrought miracles before him, with which he deceived them that had received the mark of the beast, and them that worshipped his image. These both were cast alive into a lake of fire burning with brimstone. Revelation 20:10 (KJV) [10] And the devil that deceived them was cast into the lake of fire and brimstone, where the beast and the false prophet *are*, and shall be tormented day and night for ever and ever."

After being led to re-visit these earlier chronicle editions; the Holy Spirit is now adding the next layer to these messages as a continuous flow to put the pieces of this end-time mystery puzzle together as timed released spiritually. I published some of them in my first book without this final layer before it was given to me.

First: Who or What is this beast?

Regarding bible prophecy, in my studies as now being led by the Holy Spirit, I have found that virtually, everything has happened before. We are now in the last dispensation. The Holy Spirit must be our teacher and guide into all truth that has been kept hidden from man. Our thoughts have added in imaginations where no biblical answers were given spiritually. His purpose is to help us see into the spiritual side of our purpose her on earth during our short life span here. He is the inspiration to write what God has given through man to know and save him from eternal separation. Therefore, he is the only one that can interpret accurately what all these mysteries mean in the right context for understanding sense he originally led men to write the scriptures that would be our guide to eternal life.

Second: Let's begin where it all originated in the Old Testament dispensation under law. In the book of Daniel, chapter two, King Nebuchadnezzar has a disturbing dream; in that dream, he saw a large statue whose image troubled him.

He calls all his magicians and subjects and advisors in to tell him the meaning of the dream. When they could not render the satisfaction of what it meant, he threatens them all with death. One of his subjects remembered Daniel and he enters in verse twenty-four to interpret his dream that will save their lives. The dream depicted a statue of all the kingdoms that would follow from the king's time. In the third chapter, he begins to build a stature as a memorial to his vision. When it's all completed, he assembles all to come and worship at its feet by bowing down to it during the musical ceremonies of the dedication. The three Hebrew boys refused. The king was infuriated with them for refusing to obey and ordered them to be thrown into a fiery furnace heated seven-times hotter. This is going to be their tribulation to prove whose god is their God. As you read the account of the interpretation, we are now at the time of the ten toes. This is literal under the law. After the death of Jesus, we will enter new covenant known as grace and truth, where our lives will take on a spiritual from of worship. God will now be worshiped in spirit and truth by faith; our lives as believers will be lived by faith through the unseen world in the spirit. All things will now take on a spiritual meaning after the advent of Pentecost.

The last book of the New Testament will contain the hidden mysteries to be revealed at the end of the last generation of the three sixes (representing the natural order of creation) man was given to subdue the earth. The book of Revelation will contain bits and pieces of the entire Major and Minor Prophets that will hold this mystery. At the appointed time, God will raise up prophets and messengers to interpret these mysteries. They will have the visions to the word for that time and those that receive them will be saved. Throughout times, ages and dispensations, what God has given man for good, the presents of the devil will bring him under bondage through these earthly flesh temptations.

When all is revealed, our captivity will be apparent that he has taken over the whole world including the church of Christ. **Revelation 12:9 "(KJV) ⁹And the great dragon was cast out, that old serpent, called the Devil, and Satan,**

which deceiveth the whole world: he was cast out into the earth, and his angels were cast out with him." This deception will come through men in high places … **Daniel 7:25 "(KJV) 25 And he shall speak _great_ words against the most High, and shall wear out the saints of the most High, and think to change times and laws: and they shall be given into his hand until a time and times and the dividing of time."** False teachings and new doctrines will be introduced. We all are born children of the devil as per John 8:44. The day we hear the voice of God calling us to come and claim our birthright to continue to live for eternity as His children, **Rom.8:16; …** that's when we become the new Adam, rebirth in the earth to take dominion as he did.

All who refuse to receive Christ awaits the destiny to spend an eternity with their father the devil in hell with him where embers heated seven times hotter than any fire on earth. They will spend it there for eternity in the lake of fire. Your life came from God and God cannot be killed; therefore, hell was created for the devil and his angels, all sinners (his children) will be there with him. **Psalm 14:1 (ASV) 1 The fool hath said in his heart, there is no God. They are corrupt, they have done abominable works; There is none that doeth good.**

What we will become in the future, will take place in our minds will be the war for the mind of mankind. Our transformation will come throughout these dispensations of time. When you study the scripture under the guidance of the Holy Spirit, this verse will become apparent … **Ecclesiastes 1:9 "(ASV) 9 That which hath been is that which shall be; and that which hath been done is that which shall be done: and there is no new thing under the sun."** However, under grace and truth, we have mixed law with grace. This will become the means that will cause us to live in error and not know what spirit we are of. How we will evolve into a human being controlled by a non-human entity will be one of the greatest mysteries of how over times we got to this state.

This mystery image that will cause all to be subject to it will be described in … **Revelation 13:1-13 "(NLT) 1 Then I saw a beast rising up out of the sea. It had seven heads and ten horns, with ten crowns on its horns. And written on each head were names that blasphemed God."** At this stage in the end times, Satan will have succeeded in dividing the church into body parts as separate kingdom building religions that will begin to worship in assemblies that will reflect the spirit of **Laodicea.**

This deception will represent a fall away from the apostle's doctrine. These new religions and teachings will all have one thing in common; they will claim to serve the same god without knowing what spirit the are of, therefore …

Mark 13:20 "(NLT) [20] "In fact, unless the Lord shortens that time of calamity, not a single person will survive. But for the sake of his chosen ones he has shortened those days." ...(Continue.) NLT [2] This beast looked like a leopard, (China) but it had the feet of a bear (Russia) and the mouth of a lion (America)! And the dragon gave the beast his own power and throne and great authority. This will be manifested in the form of a New World Order, the birth of the UN. ... **NLT [3] I saw that one of the heads of the beast seemed wounded beyond recovery—but the fatal wound was healed!"** This part has more than one layer, in this context, Great Britain, our mother country, nearly fell to ruins by the first of the beast systems attempt to take over the world as a form of a pre-antichrist out of German.

When Russia was invaded, we became allies and combined forces to take Germany down by the Americans invading from the **West** while Russia took the **East** segment of the country. This is what saved Great Britain from being destroyed but left her badly wounded, the help of her daughter, America. ... **NLT the whole world marveled at this miracle and gave allegiance to the beast.** The newly formed UN will set up a system that would eventually bring all nations into a one world common market. ... **NLT [4] They worshiped the dragon for giving the beast such power** (America, Russia and China will become the three major powers in the world in the last days.) **and they also worshiped the beast. "Who is as great as the beast?"**

All the nations that joined this newly formed New World Order to prevent any one nation from ever dominating the world again through tyranny. This one organization will have a secrete army and charter that will set an agenda where their end game will justify the means by which they will benefit from this new future technology that will have the potential to control the people all over the world once established ... **NLT   they exclaimed. "Who is able to fight against him?"** Once this system is in place, they will declare the age of a New World Order when George H. Bush senior as head of the western division, is elected at that time. **NLT [5] Then the beast was allowed to speak great blasphemies against God. And he was given authority to do whatever he wanted for forty-two months.** Under their charter, they will pursue authority over the affairs of the world during the tribulation as in ... **Daniel 7:25 (ASV) [25] "And he shall speak words against the Most High, and shall wear out the saints of the Most High; and he shall think to change the times and the law; and they shall be given into his hand until a time and times and half a time."** (This will be implemented during the tribulation period.) ... **NLT [6] and he spoke terrible words of blasphemy against God, slandering his name and his temple—that is, those who live in heaven.** The last president elected by the people in office will speak and declare this blasphemy against this nation; by enacting new laws against the laws of God by legalizing Sodomy.

The Christian church, divided into many denominations resulting in releasing lying spirit that will be mixed with the truth as stated in …**2 Chronicles 18:21 (ASV) ²¹ "And he said, I will go forth, and will be a lying spirit in the mouth of all his prophets. And he said, thou shalt entice him, and shalt prevail also: go forth, and do so." … NLT 7 And the beast was allowed to wage war against God's holy people and to conquer them. And he was given authority to rule over every tribe and people and language and nation. ⁸ And all the people who belong to this world worshiped the beast."** This is where this advance technology that invented the internet will set the stage for the future that will bring the world into a state of media delusion. The people in this grand puzzle, carrying strands of this DNA with a megalomania personality, will be revealed by the impact they will have on societies and governments … **(NLT) They are the ones whose names <u>were not</u> written in the Book of Life before the world was made —the Book that belongs to the Lamb who was slaughtered.** These are the people that will be martyred by them for the testimony of Jesus Christ first in third world countries and during tribulation … **NLT ⁹ Anyone with ears to hear should listen and understand. ¹⁰ Anyone who is destined for prison will be taken to prison. Anyone destined to die by the sword will die by the sword.**

This is where the Barabbas type Christians will take up arms and be killed by the same means they chose to defend themselves. As Christians, your choice will determine your fate at that time.) … **This means that God's holy people must endure persecution patiently and remain faithful. ¹¹ Then I saw another beast come up out of the earth. He had two horns like those of a lamb,** (This is America as the world's policemen in the name of Christianity; the lamb part of her disguise.) **but he spoke with the voice of a dragon. ¹² He exercised all the authority of the first beast. And he required all the earth and its people to worship the first beast, whose fatal wound had been healed.** Great Britain and the United States will be as mother and daughter. Residues of this DNA resided in Great Brittan that was present when Hitler attacked them. The internet was invented in that country but was launched world-wide by American technology. This is when the mystery of the Modern Babylon (her daughter) is revealed. She gave the world the ability to communicate all over the world and be understood in your own language in real-time. This in biblical history reveals the Mystery Modern Babylon of today spiritually. Now you remember why God had to confound them to keep them from advancing outside of his sovereign will of man's time-line to subdue the earth.

We have embarked upon the forbidden knowledge that caused the flood. What we are coming to the end of another dispensation of the time continuum, the last millennium. This new Modern-Day Babylon will introduce the spiritual form of a nonhuman entity in form of the **beast** over the airwaves that will be known as the internet. … **NLT** [13] **He did astounding miracles, even making fire flash down to earth from the sky while everyone was watching.**

This technology in the hands of evil men will be instrumental in captivating the whole world. They will be able to produce holographic images on a large scale in the sky bordering on introducing it as an ET. The Roman Catholic Church will be the responsible means to introduce the **false prophet**. In my update of how their means will justify the ends in my first book, I revealed how they will use the seminary system taught by their Jesuit priest professors to re-educate the pastors that will be sent to the Christian churches in the chronicle, **"How Satan Deceived the Christian World."** This new technology in the sky will enable them to mesmerize the population of the world by having angels in the form of ETs to transform themselves in the form of beings from another planet. They are linked to those with this strand of megalomania DNA. They are already here in operating in the bodies of men you see over You-tube pushing the people to believe science version of creation over the bible's account.

This energy, will be generated by those in great numbers, looking for this great event. Imagination is a very powerful force that by faith in a false vision can produce these kinds of false miracle on this scale. That will set up the masses to receive this grand illusion … **Acts 7:42 "(ASV)** [42] **But God turned and gave them up to serve the host of heaven:"** (Angelic beings disguised as ET's.) **Colossians 2:18 "(ASV)** [18] **Let no man rob you of your prize by a voluntary humility and worshipping of the angels, dwelling in the things which he hath seen, vainly puffed up by his fleshly mind, 2 Corinthians 10:5 (KJV)** [5] **Casting down imaginations, and every high thing that exalteth itself <u>against the knowledge of God</u>, and bringing into captivity every thought to the obedience of Christ;"** The world will be looking for something of this magnitude, their imaginations will generate the energy to produce these kinds of miracles. **Revelation 13:14-18 "(NLT)** [14] **And with all the miracles he was allowed to perform on behalf of the first beast,** (The pre-antichrist man of sin.) **he deceived all the people who belong to this world. He ordered the people to make a great statue of the first beast, who was fatally wounded and then came back to life."** Now here's the next layered revelation to that verse … we know now that the internet is the spiritual beast system, Satan operating in the airwaves as **"the prince of the power of the air." Ephesians 2:2 "(KJV)** [2]

Wherein in time past ye walked according to the course of this world, according to the prince of the power of the air, the spirit that now worketh in the children of disobedience:" This is the "X" generation that will bring about their own destruction through the use of this for- bidden technology that caused the flood. **"X"** means, they will represent the generation of extinction.

When the world-wide crash comes, the present internet system will be replaced with a new system that will be cashless when it goes online. The people of the world will be already spiritually marked as to their addiction to the internet smart phone system in their foreheads; however, the smart phone will be the device that will cause all under its power to take the mark through this device held in your right hand. This is the spiritual beast, brought to life. [15] **He was then permitted to give life to this statue so that it could speak.** All you have read is symbolic of the hidden mystery in which the book of Revelation was written that was kept from being revealed until this time in our history.

Here is where Steve Jobs will introduce the forbidden knowledge in his strand of Nephilim DNA that caused the extinction of past tribes and tongues in ancient history. This knowledge will once again infringe upon the technology that has the capability to change humanity into an in-humane existence by being controlled by an AI technology. Steve Jobs discovered a way to link the **matrix** of our brainwaves to enter your mind as a control signal, wrote an encrypted algorism in the form of an app, incorporated into his smart i-phone that will be a hand-held computer that will interact individually to your own brain's wavelength. Just like **Hal** in the movie **"2001," Seri** will now become the new upgraded reality version of **Hal's** voice you will respond too when she speaks. They will bring back an updated version of the **Pokémon** game to test the level of its control on the minds of those who respond to this app's instruc- tions. … **(NLT) Then the statue of the beast commanded that anyone refusing to worship it must die.** [16] **He required everyone—small and great, rich and poor, free and slaves—to be given a mark on the right hand or on the forehead.** All that was captivated by this subtle seduction through the internet will become the first stage of receiving the mark; now be brought under control through Steve Jobs technology to a level that crossed into the forbidden knowledge zone. …. **NLT 17 And no one could buy or sell anything without that mark, which was either the name of the beast or the number representing his name.** [18] **Wisdom is needed here. Let the one with under- standing solve the meaning of the number of the beast, for it is the number of a man. His number is 666.** This is another mystery I discovered in the spirit of truth. Satan, as the **"prince of the power of the air,"** will enter the minds of the people through this unseen spirit masquerading in the form of the internet, taking control of the world's population. This is another interesting discovery I revealed in my latest book before this goes to print.

The Pope's crown bares this Latin inscription?

VICARIOUS-FILII-DEI

The Roman numerology of this **inscription reads as follows.**

V=5, I=1, C=100, A=0, R=0, I=1, U=5

Total = 112

F=0, I=1, L=50, I=1, I=1

Total =53

D=500, E=0, I=1

Total =501

The grand total tells you who or what will be instrumental in introducing the **false prophet** whose number is **666.** The Pope in office at that time will be the one to introduce the world to this new leader of the world. All the pieces of the puzzle will come together during the tribulation when the stock market takes its final dive when God will have them pull the final plug after they have the world set to take control as the eighth kingdom of the New World Order. These new highs are designed to milk all the wealth from the financial system from those who are well connected as money become their idol and god that are not connected to their blood-line will be taken down in their greed by their own willing ignorance as they manipulate the market. They will have great financial gains by the stocks they offer to seduce them to buy. They represent the ten toes of Nebuchadnezzar's dream that will rule the world as the ten different regional divisions in the world at that time.

This advance technology will be used by the gentiles in the first half of the tribulation to judge them for infringing into this forbidden knowledge zone. The real church will rise out of the ashes of the dry bones of Ezekiel thirty-seven. It will unfold in two parts; the **first** will be spiritual, the **second** literal. When Israel rejected their Messiah under the law, a veil of darkness came between them and they are waiting for the literal return of the two witnesses in the spirit of Moses and Elijah. They will prepare them to receive their Messiah. When Satan is cast out of heaven, he will resurrect himself in the pre-antichrist man of sin when he is cut down and begin to gather the armies of the north as described in Ezekiel thirty-eight to attack Jerusalem. That's why they can't give up any land regained in the 1967 war.

They know that for the Messiah to return, they must have possession of the capital city, Jerusalem. As I have said before in my studies under this anointing, all things were happening in **"twos"** and **"threes"** as these mysteries are revealed. Many confessing Christians in my experience have not been able to receive these revelations because of long standing deep denominational beliefs that go back generations of false teachings. This I can understand; I was once in that state. The current spiritual state of darkness, currently have many assemblies blind to this third layer of the book of Revelation that will judge all that are living in this time. These revelations will require enduring the test of faith to restore the apostle's doctrine before we can be translated out of this present world; thus, ending this dispensation of grace. AMEN

On the national front

There is a great mystery surrounding the election of Donald Trump that is yet to be revealed. This is still a point of doubt for many who have no knowledge of how to read the signs of bible prophecy. Therefore, many will be caught in God's break because of unbelief. This is evident of the apostate evangelical Christian church; in their blindness, God gave them a representative of what they have become. Now this has past, I can begin to reveal the signs surrounding his administration's time in office. He is going to need prayer to restrain his actions.

1 Peter 4:17 "(ASV) [17] For the time is come for judgment to begin at the house of God: and if it begins first at us, what shall be the end of them that obey not the gospel of God?" We are entering a season of national judgment. This is our spiritual state that justifies why we must go through a tribulation period to restore divine order in the world as in the beginning of time. The church is divided into many splits of doctrinal truths that have it in a deformed state. We all are divided in part truths and therefore, only know in part. Our tribulation is to restore the true doctrine of the apostles as in the beginning. Our state is judged under this scripture … **1 Corinthians 13:9-10 "(ASV) [9] For we know in part, and we prophesy in part; [10] but when that which is perfect is come, that which is in part shall be done away."** This will happen in the first half of the tribulation of the gentiles that will be the battlefield in the spirit of the mind of every believer in the body of Christ. All these denominational kingdoms that have operated under man's doctrines of separatist movements are a direct result of our leaders that were seduced by seminary trained leadership under Jesuits professors. This is how the Catholic Church used their wealth to penetrate Christianity and got to their leaders control by what they learn in their seminaries. Our hypocrisy is now being exposed on all levels as a church, as a nation and as a government for the entire world to see. Our sins have found us out. That's why things are happening at such a rapid pace as evil man get worse and worse.

We are on the verge of becoming an extinct nation just as in the days of Noah. They had never seen rain and therefore, perished by rejecting the truth of what had never happen before. This is where you see history repeated. America has never been penetrated by a foreign country before. Therefore, she will become a victim of delusional blind pride. All these revelations that were given to me are mysteries that were held back to be revealed now. The church divided would not give place to hear the true prophet's vision to speak in their assemblies. It would expose to their supporters how they have been deceived. This is what I discovered on my missionary trip around the state of Arizona as I visited one hundred and fifty-three churches of all denominations; they are not ready to receive you if you are not well known or a media figure with credentials in the Christian community. It is a sad time to experience spiritual leaders that can't recognize the voice of God's visitation.

Therefore … **Proverbs 29:18 "(KJV) [18] Where there is no vision, the people perish: but he that keepeth the law, happy is he."** Now how many confessing Christians are happy to the point, they are ready to go home. You will find that answer in those born from above. Too often in a conversation with fellow confessing believers, they answer as having hopes for some future dreams in this world. That is evident of the deep-rooted false teachings that have blocked their minds to hear this level of truth. What's about to happen on the horizon, God must let the devil do what he has already justified that will fulfill what the prophets have already predicted in time past. Satan's agents in the earth carrying strands of this megalomania DNA are about to be aloud to carry out their master plan as the self-appointed illuminated ones **(Illuminati's)** as Satan guardians of evil in the earth that the ark angel Michael was given the authority to restrain until such a time as this.

Time for us is no more. **Daniel 12:1 "(KJV)[1] And at that time shall Michael stand up, the great prince which standeth for the children of thy people: and there shall be a time of trouble, such as never was since there was a nation even to that same time: and at that time thy people shall be delivered, every one that shall be found written in the book."** The horrors these foreigners in our government have planned for us as spies will be exposed with-out their knowing their own end will be double for double for trying to defy God's prophets. These illuminated ones behind the scenes that are in control our Congress, Senate and the presidency would not let any laws be passed concerning gun control; even during all these mass murders committed by the suicide demons released from the pit that were restrained up until this point.

They want the general population to have as many guns in your possession as you can buy so when they pull the plug, the chaos will pit neighbor against neighbor for survival and you will kill off each other in great numbers before they let the armies of Russia and China come to take their spoils. Among the communist sisters, they will adopt North Korea as their baby by making her an offer she can't refuse that will cause her to play a major part in the future. They will become the three communist sisters as a bruit beast force that will have no mercy and God will allow them to kill off 70% of the American population before he takes them out for attempting to take their Garden of Eden. **Joel 2:3 "(KJV) ³ A fire devoureth before them; and behind them a flame burneth: the land is as the <u>garden of Eden</u> before them, and behind them a desolate wilderness; yea, and nothing shall escape them."** This awaits us as a nation given over to our enemies for destruction. This is our tribulation as gentiles. This nation, at the hand of the final president, will be destroyed by meteor showers as was in the days of Sodom and Gomorrah by his predecessor's permitting the legalization of Sodomy. Our destruction as a nation, will come as an asteroid fragment that will follow the larger one that has past as a sign warning, the smaller fragment is on the way that will hit the western hemisphere and split it into three parts. **Revelation 18:21 "(KJV) ²¹ And a mighty angel took up a stone like a great millstone, and cast it into the sea, saying, thus with violence shall that great city Babylon be thrown down, and shall be found no more at all."**

The Biblical Historical background

Israel's fate began when the people wanted to be like the rest of the world; they wanted a king they could see. God warned them by putting their life in the hands of a king, they chose to rule over them will judge their nation's fate by the words and actions of that king. They chose Saul. He was handsome, well spoken, and therefore became the people's choice. Because they had been warned, in the end, as king he blasphemed the God by having that anointing on him, consulting a medium of the devil; therefore, went down in defeat. We are in this last generation with Trump as king of the free world, will commit an act of abomination against God as being arrogantly prideful. This will be our sign to the prophets of the end of the gentile age.

Now let's fast forward to the end of times and see how those that refuse to take heed to study biblical history under the anointing of the Holy Spirit are doom to repeat it. Obama was elected by the people as a symbol of hope and change. As head of this nation, he will be a symbol of a history making event. Historically, he is about to fulfill bible prophecy that will end this nation's reign as the gentile nation chosen to protect Israel. Dr. Martin Luther King became a symbol of reformation raised up by God to be a prophet to bring a warning to this nation as in the Old Testament tradition but under grace and truth.

Before he was taken out by this shadow government, he was raised up to warn, he spoke this prophecy of a dream of hope knowing that he would become a martyr. He told us what to look for when **in that day,** this man raised up would be judge by the content of his character not the color of his skin. Obama was that man that would lead us into the legalization of sodomy. Now to link this to King Saul and what he did in the beginning under the law is literally the **Alpha** & Obama and Trump will be the **Omega to** parallel the dynasty that committed this abominable act by #44 legalizing Sodomy as an elected king by the people of the free world. The other #45 will demonstrate the pride of Nebuchadnezzar that will cause God to cut his reign short by demonstrating the pride that will end the reign of kings of the free world. These two presidents, whose time to reign, the spirit that led them will cause the stench of their actions to reach God's nostrils. Obama committed an unforgivable act of blasphemy by changing the truth concerning God's creation of male and female to a lie when he endorsed the homosexual agenda by legalizing the union of the same sex and renouncing that America is no longer a Christian nation. When the Supreme Court did not reverse this decree, it became a law that spread to other states as king of the free world. Obama became the **(Omega, at that time)** the wicked leader that will cause this nation as gentiles to be brought to a sudden and abrupt end as did Saul **(the Alpha).** Israel was the beginning who put themselves under the rulership of a king they could see. Obama decreed that America is no longer a Christian nation; therefore, breaking the covenant of protection from our enemies; therefore, he will represent the end of the reign of these two chosen nations; the **Alpha** & the **Omega** coming to an end, as I have said before, Satan has justified what God must let him do through the spiritual laws of sin and death.

We are the last generation of gentiles and Jews on earth as nations, now we both as nations, are doom to repeat history. The Pharisees and the Sadducees rejected Jesus as their Messiah because they had reached the point of apostasy where they could not recognize him as their Messiah literally in the flesh. They also had become a form of religion by exchanging the law in favor of their own traditions. **Mark 7:9 "(KJV) ⁹ And he said unto them, Full well ye reject the commandment of God, that ye may keep your own tradition. Hosea 4:6 (KJV) ⁶ My people are destroyed for lack of knowledge: because thou hast rejected knowledge, I will also reject thee, that thou shalt be no priest to me: seeing thou hast forgotten the law of thy God, <u>I will also forget thy children.</u>"** This applied to the descendants of those that killed Jesus. This same word is to the church; we have evolved to where we have become forms of religions, where we don't recognize his voice when he speaks in the spirit as fallen from the true doctrine. We, as a nation only inherited what the Jews rejected … **Galatians 3:14 "(KJV) ¹⁴ That the blessing of Abraham might come on the Gentiles through Jesus Christ; that we might receive the promise of the Spirit through faith.** In 1776 that promise was fulfilled; we became that nation raised up to be responsible for their restoration the nation of Israel and their protector them from tyranny. **Proverbs 16:18 "(KJV) ¹⁸ Pride goeth before destruction and a haughty spirit before a fall."** These blessings that came with this covenant have overtaken us as a nation and as a confessing Christian church. Thus, this has now become our destiny as a once great society and nation that shall soon be no more. Let us all examine what we believe and do our repenting. May God have mercy on all that call upon his name in brokenness and a contrite heart? This is what I did when he revealed my heart. AMEN

Living in the Reality of Christ in You

Background scripture:

> 2 Corinthians 5:17 "(KJV) [17] Therefore if any man *be* in Christ, *he is* a new creature: old things are passed away; behold, all things are become new. Matthew 7:14-15 (KJV) [14] Because strait is the gate, and narrow is the way, which leadeth unto life, and few there be that find it. John 1:12 (KJV) [12]But as many as received him, to them gave he power to become the sons of God, even to them that believe on his name:"

Often in unpredictable circumstances, I experience the Holy Spirit revealing things God wants all his children to know about your unlimited capabilities He has made available to all confessing believers. Everyone born from above owns everything in the Earth. You don't have to have it in your possession. All things belong to the children of God not the devil. All that is taught in the New Testament by the Holy Spirit is for you to enjoy these blessings and not be possessed to the point that these things bring sorrows. Your priorities are set first on the kingdom of heaven because now, that's your final destiny at the end of your life. Being free indeed is not being entangled with the cares of this life that adds sorrows. Satan cannot touch you when you are in control of all you possess in this life.

That was Adam's position when God put him in charge of all he created. That's why everything in the New Testament points to you as the new creation; the Adam restored. If we use the wisdom that is found in exercising the fruits of the spirit as a surrendered vessel, you will represent the new Adam restored in full ownership of the Earth. You see, in Christ, his thoughts are higher than these meagerly elements of this world. This is Christ as the second Adam giving you the privilege through him to walk as the first Adam again. What I have learned, God has given us back the Earth and every-where you put your feet is yours because you live in the reality that He now is the greater one walking in you in the Earth.

He is calling those things as needed daily by faith to come into your possession in your daily walk. We all have an appointment with death. God has given us a time span on this Earth to accomplish what He has in His perfect will for you and He knows our departure date. All those have died before the final resurrection in Christ, that was their day of rapture for their soul. That's why He told us to be ready at any time. Only those that are alive and remain at the day of the rapture of all saints will get to see the glory we have never seen demonstrated in those saints that get to put the devil under their feet through great exploits. I cannot explain that which is beyond our level of comprehension that will be done during the tribulation.

I was watching a news clip, while meditating on what I saw, this came to my mind? Now before I explain this revelation, let me remind you that I don't think on what I see because my thoughts have already been condemned if not of God. I wait for the Holy Spirit to speak. While meditating, this is what the Holy Spirit begin to speak to my mind … *"(I have made you whole … your mind has been synced to my mind … if you can believe this, no weapon formed against you will prosper … "I AM," your creator is in you and no weapons on earth can defeat me in you … speak my word according to my will as you are led in faith, and I will perform it.)"* I have been trying to live up to that word since that day. When I made up my mind to always reply with an understanding of what the word said, I notice it has become an offense to some and a form of intimidation to others. Not being well known, most confessing Christians are not accustomed to a fellow believer with such convictions, to see him act on the word in this way. This is where you will hear some of the same words said to you as was said about Jesus. I am not that perfect yet, but I refuse to entertain doubtful thoughts God has said about this covering being in his word. All I have done is what God told all that come to him to do; believe without doubt and that did not come for me overnight. I can only say; in practice, I endured much rejection to do things His way. If I'm going to experience what He said, I must be focused on His words and His word only. I also realize why my understanding is becoming greater; He keeps adding pieces of His mind. My peace comes from keeping my mind stayed on the word in every situation. I had to learn how to discipline myself to come to this level of consciousness in my daily walk. Now let's explain these background scriptures that tell you how He (the Holy Spirit) gets our attention to walk into the perfect will of God.

Matthew 7:14 "(KJV) [14] **Because strait is the gate,** (When the Holy Spirit addresses your heart, you will become a doer of the word as walking down that road that leads to the strait gate.) **and narrow is the way, which leadeth unto life,** (When you enter that crossroad of making this decision, there will be no one there but you, God and the devil.) **and few there be that find it."** (The only way you will get to that intersection is to follow his directions in the word as you would your GPS.) **Mark 6:56 "(KJV)** [56]**And whithersoever he entered, into villages, or cities, or country, they laid the sick in the streets, and besought him that they might touch if it were but the border of his garment: and as many as touched him were made whole."** This is the road that's connected to a direct flow from the throne room through Jesus Christ to keep you perfectly whole while on this Earth as you would be in heaven and that's a promise. That's why it is your faith that keeps that flow, even when you believe in the name.

In **John 1:12,** the power of the Holy Spirit makes the connection that brings the authority not seen with the necked eye out of the spirit world where you can see what the word spoken in faith created. This is the glory of His presence in the Earth through his testimony; now in you. That's why everyone that received Jesus as the son was made whole as you would be in heaven. Now if you can believe that rather than what he, she, it or they say, or the circumstances you will find yourself in this life, will be your test to see whose report are you going to receive.

Personally, I don't want to live outside of his word; by faith, I'm experiencing him perform it to my benefit. Your choices will determine your fate which is already spoken in His word. You see my beloved brothers and sisters, that is the decision I had to make at that crossroad as to which way to turn. When I discerned who was speaking as he made known what was behind each choice, the good and the bad. Satan will not tell you the truth about where you are going; only God tells you that truth. You must learn how to discern his voice as in being born from above to receive His love. The mistakes you make along the way will be corrected as you repent and obey the leading of the Holy Spirit. This thin line of deception that will cause you not to recognize his voice comes through willful disobedience. This is how Satan gets to justify deceiving you by giving place to him as Eve did when she acted on what he said, she didn't know she was deceived until God told her what she did. Adam and Eve knew the voice of God as the first voice they heard as new creatures created in the Earth as spirit beings in the natural. Only God can open your mind to receive his words. **John 6:44 "(KJV)** [44]**No man can come to me, except the Father which hath sent me draw him: and I will raise him up at the last day."**

If we are tempted to wonder away from His presence as your covering, Satan will cloud your mind and counterfeit God's voice because you willingly gave place to him. We are warned to … **Ephesians 4:27 "(KJV) [27] Neither give place to the devil."** You have heard me speak about the sins of omission in **Gal. 5:19-21,** that's what Satan is trying to get you to do, accumulate these sins against you to justify taking you to hell before you come to the knowledge to repent. If you die in that state … **Daniel 5:27 "(KJV) [27] Thou art weighed in the balances, and art found wanting."** (This will happen at the judgment; hell is being enlarged to receive a great number of deceived Christians. **Isaiah 5:14 (NLT) [14] The grave is licking its lips in anticipation, opening its mouth wide. The great and the lowly and all the drunken mob will be swallowed up."** Among these are many confessing Christians that will be deceived by not knowing His voice when they are called to repent. That will be your day of judgment if your heart is hardened against truth. It will be your love relationship that will enable you to recognize His voice. The test may come through someone you least expect that you may be taking for granted. Don't be in that crowd of 98% of false witnesses as were the Pharisees and Sadducees to repeat history by not knowing what spirit you are of; like the leaders in His day that couldn't recognize their own Messiah, after they were told what He would look like in **Isaiah 53** and what he would do in **Isaiah 61.** Under grace and truth, those that are doers will be known by their fruit as being in him.

Often, I hear fellow Christians say to me, I'm not there yet; I say this not to offend you, but what you are saying is, I'm not ready to give up what it takes to be like Jesus. My beloved brothers and sisters, God has made it plain in His word the standards we will be judged by and it will not be by your church membership and what you did to please your leaders. Just keep this in mind; God is judging what's in our hearts that is well pleasing to Him. In my conclusion, what I see about myself, God used all my experiences, good and bad, to bring me to this present state of mind to prepare me for His calling in my life that was predestined before the foundation of the world as He … **Romans 8:28 "(KJV) [28] And we know that <u>all things work together for good to them that love God</u>, to them who are the called according to his purpose."** You may think I'm special but if I entertain that thought, I will put myself on the broad road to hell.

I have found out that to whom much is given, much will be required. He is speaking to all of us the same way. If you are not hearing like this, loose yourself from the entanglements by surrendering more of yourself as I had to do. I experience as much joy as I do sorrow and grief because of what I have been given to know and made to see. If you are being taught this in your assemblies, then we are as John said, we have this unction and will know each other when we meet, the Holy Spirit will be our witness as was in Mary and Elizabeth when they met.

In my observation of the present-day church world, the traditions Jesus rebuked the Pharisee's for are still present in today's assemblies. Any time you know what's going to happen before you get there, that's the structured order that came out of seminary train pastors. It has nothing to do with the Holy Spirit which is unpredictable when it comes to the leading of the Lord. This is the environment that contains all seven spirits in Revelation one & two that has contributed to the present divisions that has resulted in pastor's kingdom building mentality. The Holy Spirit's only purpose is to lift up Jesus and point you to the father, not man. We who are born from above worship God in spirit and in truth; therefore, where the spirit of God is liberated to heal, deliver and set souls free from sin and the oppression of the devil is where you will find those born of him from above.

That teaching from the Holy Spirit open my eyes as to who really believes the word as pastors and leaders by not liberating the Holy Spirit to take control of the assembly to have that experience each time we come together. The difference now is easily discernable, when you are a surrendered vessel coming out of the volumes of the books. A converted vessel of Christ gives the Holy Spirit the liberty to do what the father sent him to do in Jesus; this time in you. If I am willing to let him do this in me as being a converted believer that cause pastors and leaders to become offended when they see that they are misrepresenting the truth; this is what I too often will experience … **Acts 28:27 "(NLT) [27] For the hearts of these people are hardened, and their ears cannot hear, and they have closed their eyes— so their eyes cannot see, and their ears cannot hear, and their hearts cannot understand, and they cannot turn to me and let me heal them."** That's why I cannot fellowship in an assembly who is not willing to teach with convictions the whole council of the word that shows the true love for a soul that needs to be delivered. **Amos 3:3 "(KJV) [3] Can two walk together, except they be agreed?"** This is why many of us are bound by lack of knowledge by keeping the traditions of men that can lead to Satan justifying putting sickness and diseases upon us. I have found it is hard to get people in the traditional church to receive this kind of deeper truth. I have also see that there are even few that have ears to hear it unless God open their ears to it. There is an underground move back to the home church environment that is growing out of a hunger for the truth. God is leading them to come together in these last days in preparation for another Pentecost. AMEN

Now on the national front

Our nation is in a crisis condition. Biblical historians will see it being repeated as all eyes are on Israel. Her land is where God centers the activity in the world around. The reason you see so much war and rumors of wars represent God is being provoked once again to come to the aid of his people. Every nation that is against Israel in the Middle East is being destroyed by wars and the others are waiting to join the winners during the tribulation. Sense Obama pulled back on our support of Israel; this is what's causing us to experience these divisions and natural disasters. When we drew back on protecting Israel, Satan justified reaping havoc on our nation. In the end, all nations that came against Israel will be destroyed long with their capital cities. When Joshua entered the Promised Land, God told him everywhere he put his foot would become the Abraham land grant to His children. Under grace and truth, this was magnified in giving the world back to every believer as the restored Adam. In the war of 1967, they recovered their Capital city of David, Jerusalem. Now in these last days as history get ready to be repeated, all eyes will be on Jerusalem again as Satan attempts to destroy her once Modern Babylon (America) is destroyed for not protecting her.

Houston is a hub for some of the largest mega churches in America. What we see is God revealing to his people where they must put their trust. As you see, they are just self-help principal teaching assembly halls that demonstrated just where their priorities are in times of great perils and trial for his people. Now you see what they are supporting that showed no love when the test came. Therefore, we are being judged as Christians because the world is outdoing the church in taking care of their own. It grieved me to see the world criticize the church and be justified in their accusations. Why they travel in opulent luxury at the expense of robbing their members to support this co-operate kingdom building that shows no love for the poor as in self-denial. By the action of these mega assemblies who must be pressured to open their doors and share the wealth. I told you that things were going to get worst. God is going to expose them for all to see soon. I'm sorrowing to have to bring such news but there's worst yet to come. AMEN

God's Indictment to the Church

"Get Ready to Hear Final Call."

. . . .

Background scripture:

> Psalm 46:10 "(KJV) [10] Be still and know that I am God: I will be exalted among the heathen, I will be exalted in the earth." 1 Corinthians 11:28 (KJV) [28] But let a man examine himself, and so let him eat of that bread, and drink of that cup. Acts 2:40 (KJV) [40] And with many other words did he testify and exhort, saying, Save yourselves from this untoward generation. 1 Thessalonians 5:2-3 (KJV) [2]For yourselves know perfectly that the day of the Lord so cometh as a thief in the night. [3]For when they shall say, Peace and safety; then sudden destruction cometh upon them, as travail upon a woman with child; and they shall not escape."

I do not promote myself in any way because there are Major Prophets speaking under the influence of the Holy Ghost that will confirm some of these messages over the internet. In my calling, I fill in the mystery details of what we really don't want to face as the truth is revealed. My place in this wilderness is as a John the Baptist type messenger being prepared to preach for a short time and martyred during the tribulation as one of a few to re-introduce the Christ to a backslidden church. When America's economy collapses during the chaotic riots brought on by the new president's actions, the people will come to the place to see that God is their only hope. Then they will cry-out to him when they see their state with no hope left for the first time they will see what God has been trying to tell them. These are the **Barabbas** type patriot Christians who had their hopes in taking back America in their attempts to make her great again.

When they take up arms, God will give them over to our enemies for letting the devil deceive you to think that the battle was ours and not the lords. All we were asked to do as a church after the **"911"** warning was return to God of Abraham, Isaac and Jacob, He would have healed our land and exposed our enemies with-in. The elects in the wilderness are being prepared to carry the everlasting gospel of the Kingdom to be preached for the last time. Many of us will be martyred during the time of Jacob's trouble in the tribulation that many still don't believe the church will see because this mystery hidden in the book of Revelation to be revealed at that time to the end-time church age. We are in the pre-tribulation phase of this nation and the church while praying for peace and safety; we are experiencing sudden destruction by not reading the signs of the times. These signs are to tell those with ears to hear and eyes to see, get ready for we are now **"in that day"** of Judgment.

When scientist can predict a date of an event in the cosmos, it is because God has calculated everything by numbers of systems of universal changes that will return in cycles. Mankind has decoded those numbers that determine a time frame of events in the cycles of the cosmos. How are these dates significant to bible prophecy? These dates will become signs of event that will come in your life cycle time frame. The work of the prophets and messengers will tell you what to look for and at that appointed time, God will reveal the mysteries held to be revealed at that time.

The dates are on God's biblical calendar in heaven are not revealed to mankind in his natural state; only God knows those dates of a specific time of an event foretold by his prophets. It will become a test of your faith. Let me give you some human logic about time. If you knew the exact date you were going to die, you would have your bucket list of all you wanted to do in this world before that date and in your nature, would only repent on that day because of the evils with-in that would prevent you from coming before.

We are told to be always ready as having an appointment with our divine destiny, death. That is your individual day of rapture from this earth. When we go by observation as trying to predict what only God knows, this is what has contributed to the increase in scoffers by those who say they are prophets and are not, giving specific dates of things that didn't come to pass. Now the delayed signs are here manifesting in these natural disasters; here again, I see we are being set up by pre-mature sign from demonic force to captivate the world's attention at a time of this vacuum of truth. The true prophet's words are being overshadowed by all these false predictions that Satan is using to capitalize on blind zeal and people's lack of knowledge.

Mankind has been led by Satan to enter the forbidden knowledge zone, now operating among us. Man has decoded the genetic gene-splicing technology, giving him the capability to reproduce himself as a perfect natural human being, with genetically altered DNA. These genetic engineers are working on designing him to be a perfect physical human being to be programmed to do what his masters command. This was the secret work that came with those German scientists we brought to this country after WWII. They received this forbidden knowledge through fallen angelic DNA to help them become the master race people. This spirit drove them to their own destruction as God had to intervene to prevent a pre-mature apocalypse. Given the fact that the world is coming to the end of another time continuum is an indication that what they have succeeded in doing, is already among us.

Steve Job's DNA knowledge gifted him to link your brain to the internet through his smart i-phone when he wrote the algorism app that decodes your brain wave. That gave them access to areas of your brain that will control your actions. This will cause many to receive the mark through a post hypnotic seduction, except for the elects. This app is in-coded to alter a certain section of your brain's functions to follow the instructions of this beastly AI. This is the mind control they were seeking to gain over the population for mass seduction and population control. Your brain can be programmed through this electronic wavelength that's unique as your finger print. Apple's apps have the capability to make alterations to your brain wave. Microsoft created the X-Box to captivate your children's minds to take the place of the time we went out to pursue this world's goods. There again, we see these two tech giants megalo-minds effects on this last generation: Bill Gates and Steve Jobs. Apple products cause you not to be able to function without it. It's what caused you to buy each upgrade regardless of the cost. That's the danger of this forbidden technology. You will be marked in your forehead through a spirit traveling through the air over the internet, giving instructions through a device held device in your right hand. If I seem to repeat this as in other chronicles, is to drive this point home to this generation of this grand scale of addiction to your AI device before you are given over to a state of delusion to be marked for hell.

This is! the mystery of how Satan will finally deceive the whole world by coming in the form of **"The prince of the power of the air,"** This is the third layer of these mysteries of iniquity, held to be revealed now. **Ephesians 2:2 "(KJV) ² Where-in, in time past ye walked according to the course of this world,** (As a cursed child under Satan's control,) **according to the prince of the power of the air,** (Those under this influence are being used to further the cause of angelic beings using our altered DNA and our minds through electronic post hypnotic brain signals.) **the spirit that now worketh in the <u>children of disobedience</u>:"** These are the children collected by the people behind the N. W. O. which carry this gene of angelic illumination DNA. They are referred too in their circles as **"Illuminati's.** This is the last generation Satan led to be gathered in various secret scientific black opts projects we know as computer geeks with these special abilities. Only Presidents elected with this link will know of these operations. They are there to set certain things in place unknown to some past sitting presidents, using this forbidden technology that came to us through those German scientists.

Their seeds are cursed, that spirit is returning in these hate groups that carry these **swastika** and **Confederate flags** uprising in this last generation; marked with all sorts of evil tattoos and body piercings. Let us not be fools by trying to deal with these fallen angelic beings, they are spirit that was created in heaven, and you are from the dust of the Earth. Only God can deal with these principalities because he created them before they rebelled and became evil spirits. Satan is before the lord justifying taking a great deal of this last generation if we as confessing Christians fail to keep his word that would contain his activities in check.

As you see, we as a church world, fail to keep him under our feet; knowing his time is short, he asks for our children in this last generation that would release curses that would have been reversed had we remained faithful to his word as a nation. These signs would appear as literal physical marks on their bodies as a sign of this spirit. This spirit's sign will show just how strong of an evil spirits curse has over this last generation. Just look around at how many you see getting tattoos and piercings. This media technology designed to reach the masses on a large scale, will deceive you through the airwaves. Sense Satan took possession of the Earth, the only way you will be able to live the privilege given us through Christ is to let Him be in control of us. This is that unction John spoke about. **(1 John 2:20)**

We are at the stage now where if God tarried any longer, we would become godless human beings controlled by an AI, using this forbidden technology that caused the flood. The present-day church except for a few anointed pastors was conquered through the seminary system. They taught them how to use principals that cause you to escape the suffering that only reveal God's good side. These events we see are not just something that is going to go away and let our lives be the same or better; that's what the world see as their hope. Church blindness put Trump in office; he is their king Saul, raised up to lead this conservative evangelical church as their antichrist to further give his followers this false hope to think that they can **"make America great again."**

Many are under a state of delusion that caused them to believe in his lies without mentioning as **"the king of the free world,"** we must return to God as a nation through national repentance. Their election of him is evidence of the mind-set of this nation. God will now begin to expose all hidden sins of people in high places. The day is on the horizon where all alive will come face to face with these faith teachings to the point that they can't receive this revelation.

It's against everything they have been told to strive for in this world as the prides of this life. The cultural divide of races put Obama in office. He is what we got from the cries of slaves who died in hope of change. He is what Dr. King said would be judge by the content of his character, not the color of his skin. He is in a line of a wicked reign of Presidents as **"king of the free world;"** of which his predecessor, brought the curse of Sodom and Gomorrah on the nation by endorsing same sex marriage that was upheld by the Supreme Court. He was also elected by a people of color majority vote; now we have the **curse of Sodom and Gomorrah on us**. This opens the doors to all these fires around our cities that's representative of the fiery anger of God. I don't want to miss the mark by having un-confessed sins of omission; therefore, I now find myself repenting at the end of each day, things unknown to me that Satan might use to attack me by justification.

I no longer assume that I'm going to heaven, I want to be sure. Unlike no other generation before us, what we are about to face as saints and sinners alike as trouble comes on the just, as well as the unjust. Many are not prepared spiritually to deal this with-out the faith of God. We are that last generation that will be made to see what's in our hearts before you leave. These trials, we are going to face why God is exposing everything for all to see.

I strive to let the Holy Spirit bring you a soul-searching truth that will cause us all to examine ourselves while the blood is running warm in our veins. Unless pastors and leaders let the whole council of the word be declared to the people that attend your assemblies, the loss of innocent souls will be the blood on their hands. I'm not speaking to you as one who has arrived but as a fellow believer sharing with you what he is telling me out of love. We are in a race to endure to the end; none of us are walking in the full image of Jesus.

It is by His grace and mercy that he grants us this privilege. He will always address the matter of your heart as God sees you in his efforts to bring you to conviction and repentance. God does not want anyone to miss heaven with out him reminding you how he loves you by not letting you die without knowing what he really required of you. I know how blinding tradition can be; I served under it for over twenty years. It is not an easy spirit to break from when you realize you were wrongly taught. It takes a love beyond your natural feelings and emotions that only come from God to help you break from these generational attachments.

They have caused us to come short by not knowing these sins of omission by serving God on the bassist of our thoughts, feeling and emotions and not being in control of our actions when provoked by acting contrary to what we confess. I too kept God in a box until he rebuked me with a condemning word. It is not my intensions to overwhelm you or cause doubt, but this is what we should be prepared to see at this time. Many of our spiritual leaders have not taught the whole council of the truth through the Holy Spirit's perfection to believers that have this hope. We are all going to be tried for what we believe in. All the good and fond memories of innocents, good times and joys we have had the privilege to experience in this country will suddenly be gone overnight any day now. We are entering a state of sudden change seemly out of control.

All who are walking in the faith of God will get to see Him do these exploits. He will be your only hope to endure to the end. I don't have the credibility in the sight of traditional standards some of you have been accustomed to hearing in your assemblies. Having two living wives, I'm just a layman and messenger now. Therefore, I'm familiar with rejection but those of you with ears to hear, I hope you can recognize the voice of God speaking. To further explain this from the third layer context of the mystery of the scriptures, the Holy Spirit is revealing in these last days as to what's happening now. Our warning came on the soil of that nation whose towers fell on Sept. 11, 2001, her day of judgment will begin when her towers fall. **Ezekiel 26:9 "(KJV)** [9] **And he shall set <u>engines</u>** (Airplanes) **of war against thy walls, and with his axes he shall break down thy towers. Isaiah 30:25 (KJV)** [25] **And there shall be upon every high mountain, and upon every high hill, rivers *and* streams of waters in the day of the great slaughter, when the towers fall."** This describes the World Trade Towers on the lower end of the Manhattan river.

All prophecy will originate from Israel; the nation at the center of the world where all things begin with his chosen people. All gentile nations will be judged by how they treat his people Israel. Therefore, this is where we are now **<u>in that day</u>** being judged along with all the other nations as the nation raised up to protect her. Our fall will have a domino effect on all the world powers. As the Mystery Babylon (America), the third layer of this passage in ... **Revelation**

17:5 "(KJV) ⁵ And upon her forehead was a name written, <u>MYSTERY, BABYLON</u> THE GREAT, THE MOTHER OF HARLOTS AND ABOMINATIONS OF THE EARTH." The Catholic Church through the seminary system, infiltrated and changed the doctrine of Jesus Christ to where in these last days, we will become the spiritual harlot, an abomination in God's sight as also becoming a nation of Sodomites. This will only be known when she appears in that state more wicked than the one that seduced her, The Roman Catholic Church.

Rome's association with Babylon refers to her as a melting pot of all nations, tribes and tongues. She invented a system that will identify her with Babylon of old. We developed the internet; this technology gave all nations, kindred's and tongues the ability to communicate in all languages and be understood in real time worldwide. That's the mystery revealed as Babylon returns in the spirit through **"the prince of the power of the air."** That's why the word **mystery** is there. You can't associate Rome with Babylon other than being in a great nation birth with God's favor to bring her down spiritually.

According to the Jesuit's charter, **"the ends justified the means"** when President Obama endorsed the legalization, of Sodomy. Now we became the modern-day **Sodom and Gomorrah** and will suffer double in our judgment for legalizing this sin as a nation. The church embraced this spirit by many of them holding leadership roles as closet homosexuals at the time these laws were passed. That's why churches are mostly silent in a luke-warm state of not knowing what spirit they are of. We who are born from above were told to come out from among her so as not to receive her plaques. The church will be raptures before this takes place. **Revelation 18:4-7 "(KJV) ⁴ And I heard another voice from heaven, saying, <u>come out of her, my people</u>, that ye be not partakers of her sins, and that ye <u>receive not of her plagues</u>. ⁵ For her sins have reached unto heaven, and <u>God hath remembered her iniquities</u>. ⁶ Reward her even as she rewarded you, <u>and double unto her double</u> according to her works: in the cup which she hath filled, <u>fill to her double</u>. ⁷ How much she hath glorified herself, and lived deliciously, so much torment and sorrow give her: for she saith in her heart, I sit a queen, and am no widow, and shall see no sorrow."** Our pride will be our downfall by denouncing God as a nation. All will be revealed in our judgment. Here's the lamentation that applies to **America** and the rest of the world that are against Israel. This is the destiny of the spiritual Mystery Babylon, America.

Ezekiel 7:1-19 "(NASB77) ¹ "Moreover, the word of the LORD came to me saying, ² "And you, son of man, thus says the Lord GOD to the land of

Israel, 'An end! The end is coming on the four corners of the land. ³'Now the end is upon you, and I shall send My anger against you; I shall judge you according to your ways, and I shall bring all your abominations upon you. ⁴ 'For My eye will have no pity on you, nor shall I spare you, but I shall bring your ways upon you, and your abominations will be among you; then you will know that I am the LORD!' ⁵"Thus says the Lord GOD, 'A disaster, unique disaster, behold it is coming! ⁶'An end is coming; the end has come! It has awakened against you; behold, it has come! ⁷'Your doom has come to you, O inhabitant of the land. The time has come, the day is near-- tumult rather than joyful shouting on the mountains. ⁸'Now I will shortly pour out My wrath on you, and spend My anger against you, judge you according to your ways, and bring on you all your abominations. ⁹'And My eye will show no pity, nor will I spare. I will repay you according to your ways, while your abominations are in your midst; then you will know that I, the LORD, do the smiting. ¹⁰'Behold, the day! Behold, it is coming! Your doom has gone forth; the rod has budded, arrogance has blossomed. ¹¹'Violence has grown into a rod of wickedness. None of them shall remain, none of their multitude, none of their wealth, nor anything eminent among them. ¹²'The time has come; the day has arrived. Let not the buyer rejoice nor the seller mourn; for wrath is against all their multitude. ¹³'Indeed, the seller will not regain what he sold as long as they both live; for the vision regarding all their multitude will not be averted, nor will any of them maintain his life by his iniquity. ¹⁴'They have blown the trumpet and made everything ready, but no one is going to the battle; for My wrath is against all their multitude. ¹⁵'The sword is outside, and the plague and the famine are within. He who is in the field will die by the sword; famine and the plague will also consume those in the city. ¹⁶'Even when their survivors escape, they will be on the mountains like doves of the valleys, all of them mourning, each over his own iniquity. ¹⁷ 'All hands will hang limp, and all knees will become like water. ¹⁸'And they will gird themselves with sackcloth, and shuddering will overwhelm them; and shame will be on all faces, and baldness on all their heads. ¹⁹'They shall fling their silver into the streets, and their gold shall become an abhorrent thing; their silver and their gold shall not be able to deliver them in the day of the wrath of the LORD. They cannot satisfy their appetite, nor can they fill their stomachs, for their iniquity has become an occasion of stumbling."
This is the destiny of America, the Modern Babylon. Israel and America's judgment is described in Jeremiah fifty. The lamentation for them is described in Ezekiel chapter seven above. It is during this time of national morning the great revival will begin. **"Maranatha"** Come now lord Jesus lest we all perish. AMEN

Becoming one with Christ

Background scripture:

> **Romans 12:1-2 "(KJV) 1 I beseech you therefore, brethren, by the mercies of God, that ye present your bodies a living sacrifice, holy, acceptable unto God, which is your reasonable service. 2 And be not conformed to this world: but be ye transformed by the renewing of your mind, that ye may prove what is that good, and acceptable, and perfect, will of God. 1 Corinthians 2:16 (KJV) [16] For who hath known the mind of the Lord, that he may instruct him? But we have the mind of Christ. Hebrews 11:6 (NASB77) 6 And without faith it is impossible to please Him, for he who comes to God must believe that He is, and that He is a rewarder of those who seek Him."**

I have learned through the teaching of the Holy Spirit how we limit our ability to demonstrate the faith that pleases God. I have tried to be as transparent to all of you I share these messages with as to what it means to be delivered to a shameless walk with Jesus. This is what converted confessing Christian will demonstrate in your life when you are delivered from hidden prides that causes us to live hypocritical lives. You see my beloved brothers and sisters, when you get delivered from your-self, there's no more pride. This was one of my tests to see if I had been delivered. Each time you must take a stand in the word, if the world's opinion of you means more than doing what pleases God; you are still in pride. **Proverbs 21:4 "(NASB) [4] Haughty eyes and a proud heart, the lamp of the wicked, is sin."** You see how easy it is to be judged with the world by seeking their favor first? This is the luke-warn spirit that refuses to take a stand for what you know is right; God lumps you with those you chose to please. When you compromise truth to win the favor of man, you are un-acceptable to God in Christ. Therefore, when he requires your soul at your appointment with death, if you are in that state, he will spit you out of his mouth in judgment. In my observations in the spirit, I see what will cause many spiritual leaders to be lost by entertaining some form of pride that keeps God from delivering souls.

Your first priority in your salvation is self deliverance. That was Jesus' first instruction to Peter as to becoming converted. Jesus took pride to the cross to become a reproach for all who will come after him to show how pride is defeated when you are willing to be humiliated by standing in the truth. We must learn that humiliation is the only thing that will identify you with Jesus. I, for many years did not know I had hidden pride because of a false sense of humility. You can speak truth in the word without convictions and that's all it is; it stands alone until your faith is activated to bring it to past. As ministers and teachers, if we don't have convictions of who we are supposed to be representing, fear of being rejected will cause you to compromise. This test shows the loss of our first love. **1 John 4:18 "(KJV) 18 There is no fear in love; but perfect love casteth out fear: because fear hath torment. He that feareth is not made perfect in love."** Fear is a faith killer when the person speaking it shows he doesn't believe it. He does not only show that he or she is an unbeliever by not acting on what you say you believe, this is what Jesus calls hypocrisy. Your early exposure to a denominational doctrine will be known when you are asked what religion are you? If you answer, I'm a Baptist, Methodist, Catholic, Jehovah's 'Witness, Mormon or by any other name; that reply, indicates you are not aware of what spirit you are of by identifying yourself as to what you were taught to say. Now you know what I mean about being born from below in one of these separate kingdoms building denominations. All these pastors mean well as I did but the heart of the truth is where we will be judged as whether we are one in the doctrine of Jesus Christ.

Whatever spirit you have been begotten of you will speak out of your mouth. Christians convicted in truth by the Holy Spirit are identified as the doers of the word; this is where the Holy Spirit has liberty to speaks for himself. **John 17:22 "(KJV) 22 And the glory which thou gavest me I have given them; that they may be one, even as we are one: John 15:26 (KJV) 26 But when the Comforter is come, whom I will send unto you from the Father, even the Spirit of truth, which proceedeth from the Father, he shall testify of me: John 16:13 (NASB77) 13 But when He, the Spirit of truth, comes, He will guide you into all the truth; for He will not speak on His own initiative, but whatever He hears, He will speak; and He will disclose to you what is to come. Luke 22:32 (KJV) 32 But I have prayed for thee, that thy faith fail not: and when thou art converted, strengthen thy brethren." Romans 15:1 "(KJV) 1 We then that are strong ought to bear the infirmities of the weak, and not to please ourselves. John 15:13 (KJV) 13 Greater love hath no man than this, that a man lay down his life for his friends."** Our priority is to be brought to the point of conversion, so our thoughts will reflect the guidance of the Holy Spirit.

Now brother, when do you know you have become converted? When you are ready to suffer the persecutions and rejections by standing in truth? This is accomplished by studying under a conviction of love for the father like Jesus to become a doer of His word … **2 Timothy 2:15-16 "(NASB77) 15 "Be diligent to present yourself approved to God as a workman who does not need to be ashamed, handling accurately the word of truth**. (In order to do this, you are going to have to learn to?) **16 But avoid worldly and empty chatter, for it will lead to further ungodliness,"** Learning how to hear God as being poor in spirit, you will have to also learn to be quite … **1 Thessalonians 4:11 (KJV) ¹¹ And that ye study to be quiet, and to do your own business, and to work with your own hands, as we commanded you;** Never go to you work place to prove you are a Christian. This is where you must be a doer of the word by your actions. No matter what people do to you, do right to them. Your actions will speak louder than your words. This I learned when I was employed in the public workplace. I saw how your mouth in religious ignorance can cause you some un-necessary trials and the loss of your job.

Romans 12:16 "(NASB77) 16 Be of the same mind toward one another; do not be haughty in mind but associate with the lowly. Do not be wise in your own estimation." Living this principal of humble humility will change the hearts of those around you as you reply with wise council. I was trained in and institute of higher learning in one of their on-the-job training programs. It gave me the privilege to be a beneficiary of the grandfathered clause by working at an accredited institution to qualify without a college degree. I had a gift of medical insight to the human body and became a supervisor over those that did; all because of my God given talents and character, caused those around me to see what education can not give you, the ability to change the hearts of those around you by being the type of supervisor that treated his employee's with respect and trained them to become something they were not.

The increase in evil in the workplace in these last days is what I see that's bringing out this bad fruit in confessing Christians. You will be the first to lose your job by talking too much or taking matters in your own hands towards people who are not ready to hear you. Traditional church teachings have taught some of you to go out and witness to save souls. What I see a great deal is the same zeal I once had that got me rebuked by God; I was not converted to the point of being led by the Holy Spirit.

Just like Jesus knew who to tell to come as being led by the Holy Spirit, so will he in you do the same things? This is the fruit that remains as Jesus is lifted by them seeing him in you and the father calls that person into his service using your body. Everybody is not going to be saved; for those you are led to witness too, the word will either be a witness of their visitation or bring them to salvation.

Most of us never get to the third level of salvation because of the lack of knowledge from people who do not practice what they know is truth. When Jesus said … **Matthew 5:3 (NASB77) 3 "Blessed are the poor in spirit, for theirs is the kingdom of heaven."** These are the people that are not well versed in the word, but they love the lord with all their heart and that's what moves God. They may need the stability of being in an assembly; God knows them. You see, God is love and what gets his attention is when you love him back as becoming a doer of the word.

I have met people who know the word from Genesis to Revelation but have not discerned what spirit they are of; this is that lack of the convictions in their heart to let the word become flesh to where people see Jesus and not you. *What do you mean when you say, they are born from below?* They sought the kingdom through man before they sought God. Smart and well learned people will have a problem with hidden pride if not led by the Holy Spirit and that you can't hide.

Some of these are the renowned people of religious status we look up too more than Jesus because they draw the glory to themselves using the name of Jesus. I learned this, if you ever get deceived, you will never know it until God rebukes you in his love to save you from yourself. The spirit of meekness is what makes a person approachable and teachable because he or she realizes they need more of God and are open to hear his voice when he speaks. Those that get to heaven will realize for the first time what you didn't know to the point that, you will see you were just a piece of dirt God used in the Earth, redeemed by his spirit for His predestine will to be done in your body. That's why it's all about Him. If he gets to live in His image in the fulness, this is what qualifies you to sit on one of those thrones.

All you had to do is obey what he told you to do to get there with Him. Then, will you know how unworthy you were and what grace and mercy really is. God can speak truth through anybody when He opens your ears to hear Him. Their humble humility makes them takers of mental and physical abuse while at the same time loving and forgiving the abuser. **Matthew 5:5 "(KJV) 5 Blessed are the meek: for they shall inherit the earth."** This fruit is where you will see Jesus lifted to get people's attention that gives them a desire to want to be like him or get save. Sense the tragedy of loosing everything in my past including a wife; God had a future calling on my life and despite my ignorance, caused me to walk into everything he had for me to this place of total surrender and deliverance. I had to become converted first to help you see him the same way that I do; he is my everything because I am nothing with-out him.

Being rejected by my first spouse, my ignorance caused that tragedy. My present wife had to be my first convert; I am to be to her, what I wasn't to my first wife. She was religious when we met and so was I. All my focus had to be first in my home because what God had to be done was to show two not so smart people what He can do despite what people say. My priority as priest of my house was to save myself and let her see Jesus in me so we could become one together. With two living wives, I am no longer in a pulpit preacher, although I have been given the privileges to teach in few places. I claim no titles because He is able to speak for himself.

Now as a layman, I told God when I arrived at that place in her heart; I wanted to hear her say, I am her Abraham. It took twenty-five years for that to come to pass. I will never forget that day I returned home from a trip to see my mother … when I arrived home, she ran out to greet me and said … This is my Abraham. You see my beloved brothers and sisters; God called me to show this love first in my home as a doer before I could be trusted to show you how he comes out of the volumes of the books to you before He could perform what he said he will do. I too, like Abraham, waited twenty-five years for the promise to come to pass. God has done enough for me to show this reality of Himself to me. I'm just trying to help some of you get on that straight road to live the privilege of your birth-right before you leave. Perfection is an attitude of obedience to the word of God; if it were not possible to live perfect, God would not have said **… Matthew 5:48 "(KJV) [48] Be ye therefore perfect, even as your Father which is in heaven is perfect;" …** just doing what he tells you to do in His word without question is what he calls perfect in His sight because only what He said for you to do is perfect.

That's your faith speaking back to Him through you because you know if he said it, he can perform it. I learned why most confessing Christians find it hard to live this way that guarantees you victory and never defeat? Through lack of knowledge and understanding, we say we can't live perfect. This confession is why we live short of what Christ died to give us: the ability to be like Him. All He ever required is just obeying His word; then you are perfect in His sight by His grace. You must decide who you are going to serves. **Matthew 6:24 "(KJV)**

24 No man can serve two masters: for either he will hate the one and love the other; or else he will hold to the one and despise the other. Ye cannot serve God and mammon."

When you come to be converted you will see what God sees in every situation because he has your complete attention. That's when you will come to know the spirit of discernment. Being one with God is to be led to do the things he tells you to do.

You can't help everybody you see with a need, nor can you save them; this is the work of the Holy Spirit's leading. God already knows who is going to cross your path each day; that's why he told us not to take thought of the next day. You are not your own if you gave yourself back to him. Total trust is what pleases Him; the Holy Spirit is now leading you to walk down the straight road where the devil is under your feet. That's why he told you not to look to the left of to the right.

There will always be the poor as Jesus said. Learn to discern the circumstances before you give monetary support for this reason; you may be furthering the causes of the devil. When I'm approach on the street, the first thing I do is look into that person's eyes to discern their condition; then, I do as I am led. I do not give all that ask money of me. Now the word said, **"give to them that ask of thee" (Luke 6:30)**. Giving is by discernment, many are bounded by spirits of the devil and in your misguided compassion by giving them money could be the means the devil will use to take them out. Now if anybody as me for food, I will buy them some food.

Often, I'm not led to witness to some of these I see in that condition because the church is in a backslidden state. Many are being preserved for the revival to come in at the marriage supper to take the place of many confessing Christian's rejecting God's warnings to repent. That's by discernment. These are some worldly causes that we as Christian can support that the money goes directly to the people that need their help, the just as well as the unjust; **The Red Cross** and **The Salvation Army** and **your local food bank** are organizations that does not judge who you are. They are as instruments of mercy, there to take care of your needs. Let compassion be your guide in other matters as led by the Holy Spirit. We are a world in crises, and nothing is as it should be or what it seems. There are a great many needs; the begging organizations know how to use false front tactics to make you feel guilty by not giving to their causes including the church. I don't give to preacher's that ride around in private jets and limousines. I'm not their judge because God is still selecting souls of their ministries despite their error that happen to have poor people in need in their assemblies. Our riches are not measured in the wealth of this world we already own. That's why Jesus never carried any baggage, what was in Him was more valuable than silver and gold.

Our life is not about trying to acquire things we have been freely given. These things I learn by being a victim first. I see many with good intensions being scammed by the false teachers robbing you by lack of knowledge, using bible principles that work without salvation. **Luke 6:26 "(NASB) ²⁶ "Woe *to you* when all men speak well of you, for their fathers used to treat the false prophets in the same way."** The only way you will receive a crowd like Jesus, just follow his lead when he shows up healing the sick, casting out devils, and making people whole again. The reason we don't see Him manifested to this degree, we have fallen into unbelief to the point of using the principles of faith to build our separate kingdoms as parts, separated from the head of the body. We are full of religious words and medication trying to heal these parts through demons that are here to destroy what is left of us.

I had to be victimized by some of these things to be taught how to discern in the spirit. Being a friend of Christ and the Father in love is more than enough to keep you from ever being lonely. You see, he is the only one who will never hurt you, abuse you or leave you and can love you in ways that no one on Earth can. Only God can link you to a mate as an earthly companion to be of value to you while in your natural existences like that. That's why he said … **Matthew 19:6 (KJV) "6 wherefore they are no more twain, but one flesh. What therefore God hath joined together, let not man put asunder."** Our faults and shortcomings are covered under the blood as long as we forgive each-other by looking beyond them as Jesus does us and repent, as Christians … **1 Corinthians 2:2 "(KJV) 2 For I determined not to know any thing among you, save Jesus Christ, and him crucified. 1 Peter 4:8 (NASB77) 8 Above all, keep fervent in your love for one another, because love covers a multitude of sins."** You see my beloved, in the end, all is vanity when you come to this conclusion … are you standing in the God of Abraham, Isaac and Jacob as the three Hebrew boys found that came to their rescue in times of the fieriest of trials? Unfortunately, we are living in that generation that must bring back the gospel the church lost. **2 Corinthians 4:3 "(KJV) ³ But if our gospel be hid, it is hid to them that are lost:"** This time it will be our blood that will be shed in this latter rain. "Maranatha" Now may the peace of God be with you all. AMEN.

Now on the national front

In view of the coming banking crisis, I urge you to keep a certain amount of cash on hand in denominations of 1's, 5's, 10's and 20's. God does not give you a specific time frame with each word; it will be a test of obedience for a later event that all who obeys will benefit from. President Trump's actions on trade will be the catalyst that will cause many to begin to dump the dollar. Therefore, you that have, begin to help those you see are sincere as fellow sisters and brothers will be rewarded as according to what God see you need. Some of us that lack is being robbed by prosperity preachers; the poor are here to judge the rich. The Trump Presidency actions against our allies are going to cause the American dollar to be devalued up to 50% very soon. This will be that window that those with money will see God for the first time in a way they never have before and begin to help his people that have been a blessing to them spiritually. **Proverbs 13:22 "(NASB77) 22 A good man leaves an inheritance to his children's children, And the wealth of the sinner is stored up for the righteous."** This window of blessing in chaos will be from three to six months just before the economy will completely crash and marshal law is declared. Even your gold and silver will be no good to you in the crash because you will be moving into a cashless society where you will need the mark that many were seduced to find themselves already set up to receive through this forbidden technology, traveling through the airways.

Get ready for the next stage of the reality of this technology coming online in **i-phone ten computer phone.** The facial recognition technology will be the means of opening this phone, though they say you can turn it off, it's designed to profile your face when activated. This is a scene right out of the Netflix series **"Persons of Interest."** Your facial features will be sent to a government national data base to be used in conjunction with the mark.

God showed you through Hurricane Harvey why you should have some cash on hand to not only help yourself but others also. All that have their faith in God but don't have any money, what your faith in Him will do in you at that time will cause him to supply your needs. This new tax proposal on capitol hill, like Obama Care, the country has overextended the economy to the point that the current tax collection can't sustain the present economic conditions fighting two wars and the impact of natural disasters. This can not be told to the public and our current President's is a conspiracy theorist with an ego won't believe what his advisors are telling him. We are under a curse that can not be reversed. This cup of indignation is so full of evil spirits; you are going to see them manifest themselves it before you drink of it. It is sad to see well meaning prophetic teachers and religious leader trying to justify Trump's evil action without seeing that he is another tool God has allowed, being used by the devil with God's permission to speed up our destruction. **James 1:8 "(KJV) ⁸A double minded man *is* unstable in all his ways."** AMEN

Signs of the Time Series I

Past Present & Future

My messages are only a witness to the present-day church of its state. My ministry will be to those that have been reserved to replace the many that shall reject the first call to repent. It is to them I have been prepared all these years to be a harvest messenger. Those of you who read my last book should be well informed of our spiritual state as a church as well as on the national front. This follow-up e-book edition to my book titled, **"Biblical Prophetical Chronicles of the Last Generation,"** Subtitle: **Revelation; the final layer revealed."** Spiritually, if you study over these messages, you should be well informed of what God is going to expect out of every confessing Christian to endure as end-time saints. If you think we have seen the worst of things to come, you have chosen to be willingly ignorant of the signs of our times. This is the last generation of confessing believers that will have to restore what was lost in the former rain on the day of Pentecost that was delivered to the saints of the gospel of Jesus Christ.

Acts 14:22 "(KJV) ²² **Confirming the souls of the disciples, and exhorting them to continue in the faith, and that we must through much tribulation enter into the kingdom of God."** This is what I see that many are not prepared to endure. I have set grievously in prayer and meditation as Jesus let me feel a little of what he had to suffer in pain and sorrow as he saw the people turn in rejection of His message; they rather demonstrated the favor of their own traditional teachings; now brought down on the level of man's interpretation. My heart was too heavy to do any writing after that experience that seem to duplicate what we have become as a New Testament church. I have mentioned in time past, there are going to be many Judases revealed as being offended with those who will become doers of the word. This is the time you will see the reality of … **Matthew 10:36 "(KJV)** ³⁶ **And a man's foes** *shall be* **they of his own household."** God reminded me of how deep-rooted hatred can be manifested in blood lines sibling to the point of murdering your own blood as in Cain and Abel; that was the beginning.

As kingdoms rose up thereafter, this is literally what siblings did to gain power as being infected with murdering demons. **Mark 13:13 "(KJV)** ¹³ **And ye shall be hated of all** *men* **for my name's sake: but he that shall endure unto**

the end, the same shall be saved." The devil hates his own because they are in the image of God and will use them to kill all that have been given over to him. We, in America have lived a privilege that accords us conveniences that kings didn't have in time past. We are like none other; we can choose our idols, pursue them and once we obtain them, then we bow down to them in worship. Many confessing Christians are in denial as to idol worship until they must give them up is where this will be revealed in your heart. A spoil child being led by a false spirit will also have a false sense of security.

You will be a danger to yourself as well as to those around you when all he or she has lived for is suddenly gone. These sudden changes are what's activating these demons of suicide. Now Satan is using them to commit mass murder. The brute beast nature of the man in sin will show the hidden evils in his heart of a spirit he or she knows not that is with-in until it manifests. **Jeremiah 17:9 "(KJV) ⁹The heart *is* deceitful above all *things*, and desperately wicked: who can know it? Matthew 13:13 15(KJV)¹³Therefore speak I to them in parables: because they seeing see not; and hearing they hear not, neither do they understand. ¹⁴And in them is fulfilled the prophecy of Esaias, which saith, by hearing ye shall hear, and shall not understand; and seeing ye shall see, and shall not perceive: ¹⁵For this people's heart is waxed gross, and *their* ears are dull of hearing, and their eyes they have closed; lest at any time they should see with *their* eyes, and hear with *their* ears, and should understand with *their* heart, and should be converted, and I should heal them."** (When Jesus was speaking these words, they were to His own people who knew the law from memory as being taught each day in the Synagogues. They had fallen to this state … **2 Timothy 3:7 (KJV) ⁷Ever learning, and never able to come to the knowledge of the truth."** It is in this fall, many generational curse sins are revived that can kill, hurt and maim; hidden with-in, they are release under duress of extreme anger that cause crimes of passion.

I once asked why I encountered hidden anger when telling the truth; why are we seen as mean spirited or mad when we stand in our convictions of truth. His reply… **"they are holding on to something in the world they are attached too, when my spirit exposes it, this is what you see".** These are the crimes we commit when we lose our sense of compassion and love in a moment of uncontrolled anger. This is what we need to be delivered from that Jesus died to take that power over you back from the devil. There are many confessing Christians' bound in spiritual prisons as victims of being led by blind guides whose deliverance was not complete by hearing the full council of the truth with a demonstration of the power when the Holy Spirit is released.

Many with these anointings are operating in part and not in full. They have a manifestation from the Holy Spirit but what happens; we fail to continue in the truth. Having over thirty years of exposure as a confessing Christian is where I now draw my conclusions and observations by once living in error of truth, having been a victim of some of these evils from with-in me that God himself without man delivered me from for my calling. This brought me to a mature spiritual reality of things we know not about the spirit world. What convicted me, you can't defend yourself against the truth. I was guilty of hidden pride, and I didn't even know it.

That' why I speak from a transparent standpoint of my own personal deliverance experiences God open my eyes to see to enable to be used to help others see why we must first be delivered from ourselves to conversion. I have found out by these experiences, you will have to be willing to be misunderstood, humiliated, lied on, borated, and buffeted for your faults and not hold any of this in your heart against the people you are trying to help … who may be doing this to you. It is easy to say what the word said but many forget that it is God that's judging you by your actions that come out of your heart.

A few years ago, I was asked why I don't take the sacrament as those in the traditional church do. My answer: this is not a ritual to me, when I came into the knowledge of who Christ is in me, I learned I was a work in progress. I found out through the teaching of the Holy Spirit, if you are born from above, you are committed to him unto death never to turn back. Taking the sacrament under these traditional teachings can result in the transference of spirits that open you up for what Paul said about these things that will bring sickness, diseases and premature death by partaking of this in fear, doubt and unbelief. **1 Corinthians 11:24-32 (KJV) 24 And when he had given thanks, he brake *it*, and said, Take, eat: <u>this is my body, which is broken for you:</u> this do in remembrance of me.** (What is He asking you to remember? The last time I took the sacrament, I knew what I was doing. Therefore, it was at that time, I made up my mind to be faithful until death.)**25 After the same manner also *he took* the cup, when he had supped, saying, this cup is the New Testament in my blood: this do ye, as oft as ye drink *it*, in remembrance of me. 26 For as often as ye eat this bread, and drink this cup, *<u>ye do shew the Lord's death till he come.</u>** (In my convictions, I want to be available to Him until death. When you take this and mix with the world, Satan is justified in attacking you by defiling the holiness God represents. **1 Thessalonians 4:7 "(KJV) 7 For God hath not called us unto uncleanness, but unto holiness." (KJV) 27 Wherefore whosoever shall eat this bread, and drink *this* cup of the Lord, unworthily, shall be guilty of the body and blood of the Lord. 28 But let a man examine**

himself, and so let him eat of *that* bread, and drink of *that* cup. When Jesus gave the sacrament to His disciples and wash their feet, they all died at the hands of well-meaning antichrist fellow brethren to keep that sacred oath, sealed in His blood by this act. Not one of the eleven chosen, died with any of these diseases Christ delivered them from. It will be your love and faith in Him that will give him this glory until the end.) **²⁹ For he that eateth and drinketh unworthily, eateth and drinketh damnation to himself, not discerning the Lord's body.** (I don't want him to find me in unbelief, fear and doubt after partaking of his blood.) **³⁰ For this cause many *are* weak and sickly among you, and many sleep.** (Satan gets to destroy your temple by your lack of knowledge.) **³¹ For if we would judge ourselves, we should not be judged.** (When we humble ourselves to do things His way. We who walk by faith are fruit inspectors.) **³² But when we are judged, we are chastened of the Lord, that we should not be condemned with the world."** All those the lord loves as His sons and daughters will be corrected through the Holy Spirit. It will be up to those that hear Him speaking through His elect to make your calling and election sure at that time.

I have said these things before and just to remind you again in God's love. I'm speaking at the liberty of the Holy Spirit in this appeal to all that might not be prepared spiritually before the real trouble comes. One thing that is a constant reminder to keep me on the straight and narrow, every time I tend to stray being prompted by the Holy Spirit, as having a bit like bridle in my mouth. That moment always keeps me broken and humbled to want to be more like him as unworthy and wretched as some of us can be, he still loves us. Let's be honest, we are in the midst of all these temptations and only your love for God keeps you from being led astray. I ask for this to be my sign when I'm being tempted or oppressed by the devil as we all will be until the day we depart this natural body. That's why we are in a race to endure to the end. AMEN!

Now, on the National Front

Our nation is under judgment for her past sins against her citizens and to Israel. All these evils we as a people in a once Christian nation, are now being exposed on all levels in our society. This is our spiritual atomic mushroom cloud exposing all the evils of mankind at once. Satan has been given this time through this window of the absence of God in the assemblies that name his name … **Psalm 89:47 "(KJV) ⁴⁷ Remember how short my time is: wherefore hast thou made all men in vain?** (It's that vanity in our thoughts by our actions that is his window of opportunity.) **Revelation 12:12 (KJV) ¹² Therefore** rejoice, *ye* heavens, and ye that dwell in them. Woe to the inhabiters of the earth and of the sea! For the devil is come down unto you, having great wrath, because he knoweth that <u>he hath but a short time."</u>

We are that nation given this blessing to be the protector of Israel; therefore, have now violated the covenant and this is what we must face. The bible identify man created in God's image as tribes, kindreds and tongues; that's what they would be referred too after the split at the Tower of Babel. Therefore, if you are seeing yourself through eyes of race or ethnic pride, you are already in the wrong spirit. The situation in this country is going to get worst to where riots are going to demonstrate these inhumanities against each other because of these evils that have contributed to the present state of affairs to manifest this degree of enmity against each other.

Our sins of omission as a nation

1. The opioid epidemic is the curse for legalizing mind-altering drugs in a mentally unstable society. Satan is coming to take his spoils. **John 10:10 "(KJV) ¹⁰ The thief cometh not, but for to steal, and to kill, and to destroy** ... (We have let these blessings overtake us to the point that they have become our gods.) ... **I am come that they might have life, and that they might have** *it* **more abundantly."** This is our heritage we have been privileged to live, had we continued to keep Israel safe from her enemies. The kind of society we live in has become a breeding ground for all these evils. The corruption in government is going to be so obvious to all and we as a people are going to go along with; therefore, speeding up our internal judgments and collapse. **Jeremiah 50:32 "(KJV) ³² And the most proud shall stumble and fall, and none shall raise him up: and** <u>I will kindle a fire in his cities, and it shall devour all round about him."</u> These fires you see burning in California and other places are evil strong hold of Satan's Sodomy spirits. All these natural disasters will happen first on a large scale in these strongholds.

2. Because of the failure of the church to keep the standards of God' order of obedience from a biblical perspective, is in the fight for gender supremacy. The Jezebel's spirit has returned and now is being exposed through the media. **Isaiah 3:12 "(KJV) ¹² As** *for* **my people, children** *are* **their oppressors, and women rule over them. O my people, they which lead thee cause** *thee* **to err, and destroy the way of thy paths."** Our parental hypocrisy; have our children rising in rebellion. Our sins against the abuse of women and people of color by unequal justice and treating the oppressed socially by degrading the disadvantaged is returning upon us as our sins have found us out.

3. **On tax cuts;** the nation is under a spirit of delusion. We are already bankrupt. God is allowing the economy to project all these false signs to catch us in his break overnight. We all will suffer horribly in this nation if we don't wake up and repent. We will face our worst fear and see the full scope of mans inhumanity against himself. Fear of circumstances beyond our control will cause many to lose their minds and become zombie like cannibals when all food is gone. **Micah 3:3 "(KJV) ³ Who also eat the flesh of my people and flay their skin from off them; and they break their bones, and chop them in pieces, as for the pot, and as flesh within the caldron."** If they are going to be eating the flesh of God's people, we must be in tribulation. The circumstances that will cause this are explained in my latest book; **"Biblical Prophetical Chronicles of the Last Generation.** Subtitled: **Revelation; the final layer revealed"**. This will happen to the children of disobedience who will suffer the **first thunder.** When we are attacked the from East and West coast by our enemies; They are coming to take the spoils after the crash. **Revelation 18:19-24 "(KJV) ¹⁹ And they cast dust on their heads, and cried, weeping and wailing, saying, Alas, alas, that great city, wherein were made rich all that had ships in the sea by reason of her costliness! for in one hour is she made desolate.** (We, the Modern Babylon was doomed to repeat history when we set foot on the soil of Babylon of old; Iraq.) **²⁰ Rejoice over her, *thou* heaven, and *ye* holy apostles and prophets; for God hath avenged you on her. ²¹ And a mighty angel took up a stone like a great millstone, and cast *it* into the sea, saying, thus with violence shall that great city Babylon be thrown down, and shall be found no more at all.** The asteroid fragment that's on its way has been detected by scientist, it is on a collision course to create a situation like that scene in the movie **"Deep Impact"** none of you will know about it until it's too late. It will split this country in half as the Sodomy curse.) **ᵛˢ·²³ And the light of a candle shall shine no more at all in thee; and the voice of the bridegroom and of the bride shall be heard no more at all in thee:** (This will happen after the church is raptured out of her.) … **for thy merchants were the great men of the earth; for by thy sorceries were all nations deceived.** (This has reference to our CIA that started to police the world's activity by deceiving our allies until we were exposed as to what we were doing that God could no longer protect us in our evil state.) **²⁴ And in her was found the blood of prophets, and of saints, and of all that were slain upon the earth."**

Just like the Babylon of old did not exist after her fall any more by name; neither will we anymore as a nation after the tribulation. There will be nowhere to run or hide outside those who are under divine protection to repopulate the millennium and those used to glorify God during this time will demonstrate great exploits against the antichrist.

Ninety-eight percent is going to reject the call among the confessing church-world just as the Jews rejected Jesus as their Messiah; the church will repeat history by not knowing his voice of warning through his messengers. They will be replaced by those in the highways and by-ways better known as the homeless, pimps, prostitutes, body art piercing and the scum of the earth will take their place at the marriage supper of the lamb. That parable is a prophecy to be fulfilled during the great revival. **Luke 14:21 "(KJV) ²¹ So that servant came, and shewed his lord these things. Then the master of the house being angry said to his servant, Go out quickly into the streets and lanes of the city, and bring in hither the poor, and the maimed, and the halt, and the blind."** God will open their hearts to receive this last everlasting gospel and be saved. It is evident that hell is being enlarged during these natural disasters as seen when many volcanos begin to erupt. **Isaiah 5:14 "(KJV) ¹⁴Therefore, hell hath enlarged herself and opened her mouth without measure: and their glory, and their multitude, and their pomp, and he that rejoiceth, shall descend into it."**

Dearly beloved, what the Holy Spirit has revealed to me by way of these media revelations are the bassist of all my writings to this end-time generation to help those with ears to hear and eyes to see, save yourself from what is inevitably on the horizon any day now. Therefore, all these sayings will be tested by the spirit of prophecy in the days ahead as to truth to who are the real prophets and messengers of God. **"Maranatha"** My prayer in faith is that none of you that got to read this vision be lost. Whether you believe it or not, we are approaching **the end of the gentile age.** AMEN

Signs of the times II

The Reality of the Spirit World

* *

Background scripture:

> 1 Chronicles 10:13 (NKJV) [13] So Saul died for his unfaithfulness which he had committed against the LORD, because he did not keep the word of the LORD, and because he consulted a medium for guidance. 1 Chronicles 10:13 (NLT) [13] So Saul died because he was unfaithful to the Lord. He failed to obey the Lord's command, and he even consulted a medium."

In rightly dividing the word, one must have and understanding of the spirit world and a revelation of the law of **the spirit of life and the law of sin and death**. In this scripture, I will use Saul as an example to make this point. Consulting with a medium under the law was forbidden by God's chosen people. The consequence is sudden death because the Holy One (God) is blasphemed by having this distinction and resulting to seek out Satan for and answer.

Communicating with the dead is forbidden; even pagan worship of dead relatives in the underworld is forbidden in the sight of God. Such practices are of the world as the children of the devil. There's a forbidden zone of communication; a guff between Paradise and hell. Saul violated the law of sin and death with the anointing of God on him when he sought to consult with Samuel's spirit through a medium in the underworld. Samuel was not in hell but in paradise; therefore, God intervene by bringing up Samuel's spirit which judged and condemned him for breaking the law of sin and death by consulting a medium as an anointed vessel; therefore, sealing his fate in hell.

The present-day church world under the influence of familiar spirits is blind to these realities by only knowing in part. The fullness of Christ is where all things are known. Not many confessing Christians are in that place of conversion to discern these spirits operating in your midst. Case in point, I once was in a meeting with some fellow saints: one of the brothers confessed he had permitted his girlfriend as a sinner to have an abortion. The next thing I hear and see is one of the spiritual women telling him that his aborted daughter was standing there beside him as a young girl.

Even I did not understand it until later one of the brothers said the Lord had revealed to him that this was a form of witchcraft. If you are not living to die from this world, it is evident you are in love with the world that contains these spirits operating among the people. That's why He said … **1 John 2:15 (KJV) "15 Love not the world, neither the things that are in the world. If any man love the world, the love of the Father is not in him. Matthew 7:21 (ASV) 21 Not everyone that saith unto me, Lord, Lord, shall enter into the kingdom of heaven; but he that doeth the will of my Father who is in heaven. 1 Timothy 4:1 (ASV) 1 But the Spirit saith expressly, that in later times some shall fall away from the faith, giving heed to seducing spirits and doctrines of demons, Ephesians 5:11 (KJV) 11 And have no fellowship with the unfruitful works of darkness, but rather reprove them."**

This is Satan in disguised as an angel of light dispensing religious spirits in those who follow these false teachers under the influence of these demons. This is evident by having no standard of holiness. That's why we can't seem to get along as confessing Christians because these spirits have their own personality and agendas by only knowing in part until that which is perfect returns. **(1 Cor.13:9,13:12)**

There is no oneness in operation and the fruit is contrary to **Gal. 5:22-23.** I have been around long enough to see the fall of some of these men being seduced by these spirits claim to have had a visitation in heaven. When one is truly born from above, he will show a sign of his conversion. Their spiritual DNA is length to the host in heaven. Your mind is set on heavenly things. This is when you are a convert. **John 3:12 (ASV) "12 If I told you earthly things and ye believe not, how shall ye believe if I tell you heavenly things?"** Only God knows himself in the spirit. This is that unction in all who are converted as he told Peter in … **Luke 22:31-32 (ASV) "31 Simon, Simon, behold, Satan asked to have you, that he might sift you as wheat. 32 But I have prayed for thee, that thy faith fail not: and when thou art converted, strengthen thy brethren."**

This is the work of Christ at the right hand of the father, selecting souls to be added to the kingdom. A remnant has been taken from each time, age and dispensation; therefore, no one can pluck them out of God's hand. (John 6:44) Satan's mediums can only operate in the realm of the souls appointed to hell;

therefore, if one consults a medium and that person's voice answers through the medium, they are in hell. Remember, the medium Saul consulted was in great fear when she saw in her spirit the hand of God crossed over into the forbidden zone to Paradise to bring up Samuel. People with strong soul ties to worldly things and people are candidates for these seducing spirits. Therefore, Jesus tells us … **2 Corinthians 6:17 (KJV) "¹⁷Wherefore come out from among them, and be ye separate, saith the Lord, and touch not the unclean thing; and I will receive you,"** There are religions of cults that have people bound under the law in false teachings. If you are born from above, you will not keep company with the worldly who may practice such things as consulting with mediums and those who deal in the arts.

I was asked about cremation for Christians; Let me give you some sound revelation on this subject. Your body came from the dirt, the only reason we can see each other, is because we live in a natural body. When one dies, the manner or the conditions that took them out could mean, there's no body to be resurrected if it was consumed by some beast to tragedy, so what is being resurrected? The sole of your existence is what's being resurrected by God is what's being judged, that's what has to give an account of your existence, not your natural body.

Soul bonds are evident when the person can not let go biological or spiritual bonds that has him or her in bondage to their spirit. This type of seduction will blind your state of conscious reasoning. That's what cause you to not be able to let go when you are being abused against your will. These are mostly things that have life in them that lead you to idol worship. When one meditates on what dominates their thoughts, if these thoughts are evil, Satan will turn your thoughts into imaginations and a desire to be with that person or thing. That's why the scripture say … **Matthew 5:28 (KJV) "²⁸But I say unto you, that whosoever looketh on a woman to lust after her hath committed adultery with her already in his heart. Proverbs 23:7 (KJV) ⁷For as a man thinketh in his heart, so is he: Eat and drink, saith he to thee; but his heart is not with thee."**

When one gives his heart to another, he or she will live for that person in a soul bond tie that can make them inseparable, even in death. As I have said before, Satan duplicates what God does because he knows nothing new. When we become new creatures, we have a soul tie to the Father and the son.

His spirit has taken over our souls. These spirits are among you in your in un-regenerated family members and friends. That's why Jesus said …**Luke**

12:53 (KJV) "⁵³ The father shall be divided against the son, and the son against the father; the mother against the daughter, and the daughter against the mother; the mother in law against her daughter in law, and the daughter in law against her mother in law. Matthew 10:36 (NKJV) ³⁶ and 'a man's enemies will be those of his own household. Luke 14:26 (NLT2) ²⁶ If you want to be my disciple, you must hate everyone else by comparison— your father and mother, wife and children, brothers and sisters—yes, even your own life. Otherwise, you cannot be my disciple."

Only God in you can convert your family members. This passage of scripture above underlined; I must explain; the word **hate** in this context has reference to people in your immediate family that continue in sin as try to persuade you to continue with them. Your friends are included in this also who may be of your past life in the world. You don't hate them but the sin nature that seeks to oppress you.

There's difference between holy and unholy. When one is converted, God can add all in that person's life what they need to keep them in his perfect will. When God takes over your life, He will transform your life to His perfect will. Now, this brings us to see the two parallels in the spirit world. Satan duplicates everything God does; the difference, you will never know when you are deceived until God opens your eyes and ears to truth. Most of us as Christian converts are raised in some form of spiritual error as evident when we can't agree in matters of truth. **Amos 3:3 "(KJV) ³ Can two walk together, except they be agreed?"** Remember, the Pharisees did not know what spirit they were of when Jesus told them they were of their father the devil. **John 8:44 (KJV) "⁴⁴ Ye are of your father the devil, and the lusts of your father ye will do. He was a murderer from the beginning, and abode not in the truth, because there is no truth in him. When he speaketh a lie, he speaketh of his own: for he is a liar, and the father of it. Luke 9:55 (KJV) ⁵⁵ But he turned, and rebuked them, and said, Ye know not what manner of spirit ye are of."** It is not my intentions to cause you to doubt your salvation; these are some of the spiritual truths we missed by lack of right revelation knowledge that cause us to be divided.

Those who worship God in spirit and in truth know the destiny of all who die in him will live for eternity. The Holy Spirit of God does not seek to bring back spirits from heaven once you cross over in the shading of the fleshly body of this world. The clinical death experience is an act of mercy from God to reverse the decision of Satan to continue that person's life for God's purposes, not the devils. Satan will try to take you out before your time. There is no communication in the afterlife for those in the third heaven. Even there, we are as angels and will not relate to each other as we did here in the flesh; so don't think you are going to be like you were here in the Earth there.

On the other hand, if Satan has seduced you to serve another god while being a confessing Christian, this will be the void you seek to fill when your idol is gone, remember, **"Thou shall have no other gods before me."** We don't see them as other gods because we think what we are doing is alright. You are in the realm of the carnal that deals in feelings and emotions. This type of deception gets us condemned for eternal separation by committing sins of omission. If we die in that state. **Proverbs 16:25 (ASV) "25 There is a way which seemeth right unto a man, But the end thereof are the ways of death. Hosea 4:6 (ASV) 6 My people are destroyed for lack of knowledge: because thou hast rejected knowledge, I will also reject thee, that thou shalt be no priest to me: seeing thou hast forgotten the law of thy God, I also will forget thy children."** If you have been taught wrong, you will cause that spirit to be in your children. Therefore, your children will be judged under that same curse.

There are seventeen sins in **Gal. 5:19-21** in the KJV, if you die in any one of these as a confessing Christian, you will not enter heaven. The cause of most of our grief is due to too many worldly attachments. As confessing Christians, if we don't obey the word of God, and choose to compromise the truth, we spread these spirits to our children who in return will rebel against us later when they discover that you are living in a form of hypocrisy. You can not love the world and God too. **2 Timothy 2:4 (ASV)" 4 No soldier on service entangleth himself in the affairs of this life; that he may please him who enrolled him as a soldier." 2 Corinthians 6:14 (KJV) 14 Be ye not unequally yoked together with unbelievers: for what fellowship hath righteousness with unrighteousness? and what communion hath light with darkness?** You are the property of God; in his army, your rewards will not only be the spoils of this life in the victories over the devil, but even greater in heaven. When some one close to us in the flesh dies in sin … yes, it's grievous because you know that person will be separated from God for eternity. These new doctrines that teach us that we are all God's children and will be forgiven after you die in sin, is where Satan tells us that he or she is in heaven because we were convicted in a religious spirit that tell us what we want to hear. Remember, Satan is the spirit of religion not salvation.

This spirit makes you feel comfortable keeping company with your worldly friends. Some of these have created a cult like following that have separated themselves from all else to practice a form of the law of the word. Where there's no Jesus, it becomes a religious form under the law. This is a carry over from the Pharisee's teaching under the law of separatism. They rejected Jesus and expelled anyone who followed him. It then becomes a cult with-out the love of Jesus. Satan will have you manifesting a counterfeit love. They only see Jesus as a prophet like Elijah, not the son of God. We see this demonstrated in religious movements such as Jehovah's Witnesses, Mormonism, and followers of Islam religions and Sabbath day only worshippers. This in part is due the error in interpretation of scripture by mixing law with grace, usurping law over grace that makes the people you convert into two individuals … **Matthew 23:15 "(NKJV) ¹⁵ Woe to you, scribes and Pharisees, hypocrites! For you travel land and sea to win one proselyte, and when he is won, you make him twice as much a son of hell as yourselves."** … They are denying that Jesus came not in flesh while keeping the law which will make you a judge of others that shows no mercy or love like a Pharisee.

This is the part that sees Jesus as a prophet not the son. Just as Jehovah's witnesses believe that Paradise is heaven on earth that all who believe, just be as good as you can. This teaching that tells you no one can live perfect in this world and continue to say we are just sinners and God will have mercy on us while we continue in sin; therefore, all will be raised up perfect to live in paradise which they say comprise the numberless multitude; to them, this is their new heaven on earth. That's what I was told many years ago when they tried to convert me.

Another observation I see, those who mix law with grace have a tendency to judge others. **2 Corinthians 6:17 (KJV) "¹⁷ Wherefore come out from among them, and be ye separate, saith the Lord, and touch not the unclean thing; and I will receive you."** We see in the gospels, when Christ went before the sinners, it was not to participate in their sins but to show them the father and call those out the ones the father has chosen.

A religious person confessing to be a Christian may not know their soul ties until that person or thing is severed from your life; if you have never renounced this tie, its effects will become apparent at the time of the lost. This is what we see when a sudden change, brought on through circumstance that triggered you to react to this degree of a change in character. This becomes the void you seek to fill in that lingering state; seeking answers to things you refuse to accept. This is what lead you to consult a psychological medium for mental help. We who are Christians indeed are not ignorant of these circumstances of this life. We see things as they **are,** and not what we imagined them to be. If the death of someone closer to you than Christ and that person's spirit is constantly calling to you, this is evident that you are entertaining a soul tie. It is the worldly that seeks a medium, not a Christian.

You can live that close to God that he will reveal the manner of your departure, but this will never happen until your mind is in heavenly places in Christ. You need to renounce that spirit and ask God to forgive you for letting the loss of that person or thing, take his place. Christ has redeemed us from the curse of the law of sin and death. When we know this is our destiny; **Hebrews 9:27 (KJV) "27 And as it is appointed unto men once to die, but after this the judgment:"** Death in Christ becomes a joyous home coming to the saints to see a fellow sister or brother leave the troubles of this world. Jesus wept for a moment when Lazarus died. The cross of Christ gave us the right to claim our birth right after having committed the most heinous of sins, just by confessing them through repenting we receive forgiveness. Now forgive yourself and go and sin no more.

Many of us have been married more than one time as Christians, this under grace and truth is permitted until one comes to the knowledge of the truth. The woman at the well was not convicted until she asks for that living water; that's when she came face to face with the truth, Jesus. Up until that time, she was an outcast among her own because of her sins. **John 4:11 "(KJV) 11 The woman saith unto him, Sir, thou hast nothing to draw with, and the well is deep: from whence then hast thou that living water?"** When Jesus offered her that living water, she had to confess her sins of adultery; that's when she came to the knowledge of truth.

Until you come to the knowledge of truth, sin will reign in your mortal body until you are convicted. If you are partially subject to the word of God, you will be partially subject to each other in marriage and friendships. As a confessing Christian, no matter what you speak in truth, the substance of what you do will speak louder than your words. God has not changed his qualification for leadership under the ministerial graces; **(Eph. 4:11-12)** as we are told in the book of 1 Timothy; therefore, you can work as an obedient servant and be as effective as one with the Godly qualification because God is no respecter of persons. Having a second living wife would be a reproach under grace and truth as a pastor. This will not keep you out of heaven because under grace and truth, He seeks out those who will do his will, titles are not important to God; only in your willing obedience, he gets to speak for himself.

You don't need a title to be used of God; however, the qualification to hold a position of leadership has not been compromised by God. The lack of convictions to truth has caused us to operate in the permissive will of God. Therefore, these reproaches will follow you. There is no greater sin than letting someone or something become your god. Many of us will never see the truth until the real gospel is preached again in the purity and power of the Holy Ghost with signs, wonders and miracles following as having Christ returned to perform the greater works as now will be in the latter rain. That's why there must be a period of tribulation, to clear up this mess we have made in division to see who the real God of Abraham, Isaack and Jacob is.

I have learned this from the teaching of the Holy Spirit, our state under grace is mercy indeed. Just as I had to be told to quick thinking and surrender my will to activate the Holy Spirit; this is when I saw myself as becoming a little man child with a teachable spirit, then I begin to see what God sees. We will be judged by what His word has said and not one word will be compromised. All He has said in His word is what we will be judged by as what He required. **Matthew 4:4 (KJV) "⁴But he answered and said, It is written, Man shall not live by bread alone, but by every word that proceedeth out of the mouth of God."** That means whatever we have learned, that we must do. The way to Christ is through the draw of the Holy Spirit; he is your master teacher. I have come to see that the heart of man is wicked and only God can tame it.

The reason why we fall short, the flesh has a will and desire of its own; even as Christians, we war with this daily. When we gave place to seducing spirits that brought parts of our flesh to life, they will take control of our thoughts that reveal what spirit we are of when we are provoked. The real gospel, preached under the anointing of the Holy Spirit, searches out these deep-rooted spirits and expose them to your conscious state; then the hidden man of the heart that was there when God breathe him into Adam, now can convict you of your state before God. He represents the mind of God that has judge your state as a sinner, shows you the only way you will be able to get back in right standing with God is to repent. **Luke 6:46 "(KJV) ⁴⁶And why call ye me, Lord, Lord, and do not the things which I say?"** This will be the sign of those chosen by God unto election that will preach and teach the real gospel. They will do what God say because they were given ears to hear and be convicted. **John 15:16 (KJV)¹⁶Ye have not chosen me, but I have chosen you, and ordained you, that ye should go and bring forth fruit, and that your fruit should remain: that whatsoever ye shall ask of the Father in my name, he may give it you. Matthew 7:21 (KJV) ²¹Not everyone that saith unto me, Lord, Lord, shall enter into the kingdom of heaven; but he that doeth the will of my Father which is in heaven.** The uncompromised walk is by election because flesh and blood can not serve God ... **John 4:24 (KJV) ²⁴God *is* a Spirit: and they that**

worship him must worship *him* in spirit and in truth. John 4:24 (NASB) ²⁴ "God is spirit, and those who worship Him must worship in spirit and truth." John 4:23 (KJV) ²³ But the hour cometh, and now is, when the true worshippers shall worship the Father in spirit and in truth: for the Father seeketh such to worship him. 1 Corinthians 15:50 (KJV) ⁵⁰ Now this I say, brethren, that flesh and blood cannot inherit the kingdom of God; neither doth corruption inherit incorruption.

It is a religious person that serves God out of a carnal mind which represents a lack of convictions to truth; they just are not ready to fully obey so they serve God on their terms. This will also be manifested in our walk as a lack of knowledge of truth by not understanding of what God requires. **John 6:44 "(KJV) ⁴⁴ No man can come to me, except the Father which hath sent me draw him: and I will raise him up at the last day."** All of us are given the right to claim our birth right through those chosen by election as were the original apostles. Those with ears to hear will receive them and make their calling and election sure. In the type and shadow of the old covenant, those that heard and obeyed God through Moses went into the promise land which in the end were only their children, Joshua and Caleb; All were left to die in the wilderness for falling away from the God that showed the who He really is. **Matthew 24:13 "(KJV) ¹³ But he that shall endure unto the end, the same shall be saved."**

The great fall away is due to there are not many elected as ensamples to keep God' presents before the body confessing to be of Christ. The time God takes to get you here, you may find it is very few. That's why in our time of the end, this gospel that has been lost will be preached to them that are lost that the church fail to reach. We in the confessing Christian church-world have had two thousand years to get it right. Now we are in a state … **Isaiah 53:6-7 "(KJV) ⁶ All we like sheep have gone astray; we have turned everyone to his own way; and the Lord hath laid on him the iniquity of us all. 2 Corinthians 4:3 (KJV) ³ But if our gospel be hid, it is hid to them that are lost:"** This is the degree of deception that has resulted in this time of willing ignorance which has been the grief of God, **(the father of all creation)** to have to suffer many souls to be delivered unto their father they chose, when they were warned. They will meet his fate as children of the devil. (John 8:44) May God open your eyes to see the times you are living as this being a warning; for some it will be our last. May God have mercy on all that call upon His name. AMEN

Signs of the Times III

The Unseen World of the Spirit

Background Scripture:

> **1 John 4:1 (NASB) [1] "Beloved, do not believe every spirit, but test the spirits to see whether they are from God, because many false prophets have gone out into the world. Matthew 24:5 (NASB) [5] "For many will come in My name, saying, 'I am the Christ,' and will mislead many. 1 Timothy 4:1 (NASB) [1] But the Spirit explicitly says that in later times some will fall away from the faith, paying attention to deceitful spirits and doctrines of demons, Ephesians 5:11 (NASB) [11] Do not participate in the unfruitful deeds of darkness, but instead even expose them;"**

The unseen world of the heavenly host is not visible to the natural man. Adam's creation was natural in the body form but spiritual in his existence. He had no concept of his natural state of his physical being until he sinned. He walked in the spirit daily and commune with God as one in spiritual accord. It was not until he sinned that he left his spiritual state, now a veil will separate the spiritual part of him from God.

This veil severed their spiritual communion and put all that came from his seeds under a curse as a child of the devil. He could no longer see or walk in the spirit as before he sinned. Mankind was reduced to a natural brute beast as were all the other animals in God's creation. The harmony became enmity. Satan dethroned in heaven now had succeeded in gaining access to this world through the fallen state of man. He had no access to manifest himself in because he must have something with life from God to transfer his spirits.

This access will provide bodies to these fallen disembodied angelic spirits. When Adam sinned, this gave them access to enter man and all created things through their seeds being defiled that will be manifested down through times, ages, and dispensations including the cosmos and the universal things. All those born after Adam's sin will be under a curse as the children of the devil.

(John 8:44) God's plan of redemption is in his sovereign will, ordained before the foundation of the world, set in motion before the presents of established evil; God foreknew all things and set them to run their course throughout time from the end back to the beginning. **Isaiah 46:10 "(KJV) ¹⁰ Declaring the end from the beginning, and from ancient times *the things* that are not *yet* done, saying, My counsel shall stand, and I will do all my pleasure:"**

Throughout time, He will select his remnant during man's time on earth that will comprise the heavenly host of saints redeemed to live for eternity. The first stage of God's mercy on man is stated in the law of the old covenant as conditions under which his chosen people are acceptable in his sight. The mystery of iniquity will be the revelation to man of the unseen powers in the spirit world that will be at war with-in his mind daily for his soul.

The knowledge of good and evil will be determined by the choices he makes by use of his free-will. Man's obedience to the law in the old covenant and by faith in the spoken word after the resurrection of Jesus Christ will be contained in these two covenants. Until the advent of Jesus Christ, the sin nature, even under the law did not keep him from the sinning in the flesh. Satan's power over mankind will be in rejecting the Commandments of God. Man's ignorance of the spirit world will cause him to live beneath his privilege as a confessing child of God. The revelation of the spirit world after the resurrection of Christ will give men the ability under this new covenant to live a sinless life in Christ. The re-created God man is Christ in you to restore the glory of the father in the regenerated souls of men; the new Adam. The revelation of Jesus Christ will give all who received him the power to become the sons of God. This warfare will border on the knowledge of good and evil which we now have to deal with two thoughts, the knowledge of good and evil; the ramifications of your choices will dictate the consequences of our life circumstances. God will use these circumstances to perfect our faith; lack of this knowledge will cause many to lose their birth right.

Hosea 4:6 "(KJV) ⁶ My people are destroyed for lack of knowledge: because thou hast rejected knowledge, I will also reject thee, that thou shalt be no priest to me: seeing thou hast forgotten the law of thy God, I will also forget thy children." The fall of man put him in a double minded state unstable at his best by not knowing what spirit he is of.

Apostle Paul came to the knowledge of these two natures that's at war against the will of God in us all. **Romans 7:15-25 "(KJV/NLT) ¹⁵ I don't understand myself at all, for I really want to do what is right, but I don't do** it. Instead, I do the very thing I hate. ¹⁶ I know perfectly well that what I am doing is wrong, and my bad conscience shows that I agree that the law is good. ¹⁷ But I can't help myself, because it is sin inside me that makes me do these evil things. ¹⁸ I know I am rotten through and through so far as my old sinful nature is concerned. No matter which way I turn, I can't make myself do right. I want to, but I can't. ¹⁹ When I want to do good, I don't. And when I try not to do wrong, I do it anyway. ²⁰ But if I am doing what I don't want to do, I am not really the one doing it; the sin within me is doing it. ²¹ It seems to be a fact of life that when I want to do what is right, I inevitably do what is wrong. ²² I love God's law with all my heart. ²³ But there is another law at work within me that is at war with my mind. This law wins the fight and makes me a slave to the sin that is still within me. ²⁴ Oh, what a miserable person I am! Who will free me from this life that is dominated by sin? ²⁵ Thank God! The answer is in Jesus Christ our Lord. So you see how it is: In my mind I really want to obey God's law, but because of my sinful nature I am a slave to sin."** These scriptures by interpretation, Paul is acknowledging the ramification of his actions and ours that have a tendency to act contrary to the will of God.

This is where Paul received a revelation of who is with-in you that gives you the ability not to willfully commit sin. Without a revelation of the above Scriptures, we will continue to confess our infirmities; saying, we can't live perfect when the Scripture say to the contrary in… **Matthew 5:48 "(NLT) ⁴⁸ But you are to be perfect, even as your Father in heaven is perfect."** What Paul was describing is the nature of the old man of sin under which curse we were all born. The power to live perfect will require a revelation of who will in able you to live perfect by and through perfect obedience to God's spoken word. The Holy Spirit will give you this power to continue to live in this world and no longer be of it. **2 Corinthians 5:17 "(KJV) ¹⁷ Therefore, if any man be in Christ, he is a new creature: old things are passed away; behold, all things are become new".**

Our love for Christ will determine our degree of perfection. What this mystery will reveal is total surrender to the will of God. Under grace and truth, we can now live perfect. The reason we can not see how this is possible, we have not been convicted by Godly in-samples when the gospel is preached in the purity and power of true holiness through the inspiration of the Holy Spirit that brings deliverance to them receive him. The Holy Spirit gives this power to as many as received Christ the ability to live perfect in spirit, soul, and body.

It is he that will bring all things to your remembrance by receiving the engrafted word of God. Don't try to do this in your own strength; this is why you must have that child-like faith that doesn't question him. The word teaches us to die daily from that old sin nature to be replaced by the God nature. This process in our salvation is the transition period of which will be according to your obedience to walk the straight and narrow road to perfection. **(Matt. 7)**

When Adam and Eve sinned, the knowledge of good and evil cause them to be in a state of confusion. This was because they had no knowledge of evil. The evil nature they inherited when they broke the law of sin and death; now they will be given over to seducing spirits and demonic influence released into God's creation and beings. This is the great mystery of iniquity; Satan now has the power to enter God's creation by reasons of Adam' fallen state through his seeds. These fallen angelic beings now have at their disposal the bodies of all living creatures. **Colossians 1:16 "(KJV/NLT) ¹⁶ Christ is the one through whom God created everything in heaven and earth. He made the things we can see and the things we can't see—kings, kingdoms, rulers, and authorities. Everything has been created through him and for him."**

The great mystery of iniquity will be manifested in all living creatures; therefore, defiling all God's creation. These demonic spirits will be seen in everything that God has created far good will now be used for evil. This is where we need the revelation of the spirit world and who is at war in your members, causing you to do good and evil at the same time while striving to serve God through a sincere conviction of sin. This unseen spirit world will be seen as … **Ephesians "(KJV) ¹² For we wrestle not against flesh and blood, but against principalities, against powers, against the rulers of the darkness of this world, against spiritual wickedness in high places."** Why does man have to have something to serve, it is his inherent nature to serve something other than himself. Now the gods of this world will be the things he will seek to serve through the lust of the eye, the lust of the flesh, and the prides of life. This is the nature of the evil man controlled by his father the devil who' soul is now in his possession by birth under the curse pronounced on Adam and Eve. He will have the ability to gain the whole world and still end up in the lake of fire with his father, the devil.

Now what I am about to reveal to you may cause many to be offended given the revelation of whom or what you are now in servitude too. **Exodus 20:3 "(KJV) ³ Thou shalt have no other gods before me."** All of God's creation is at Satan's disposal. As natural brute beast, we will be victims of seduction through our five senses. Our choices will be influenced by our emotions dictated by the circumstances of life. Satan, as his child, will show you the kingdoms of this world under his possessions to choose from as his servant; including the false churches he will establish in the name of religion. He will offer you what he offered Jesus in … **Matthew 4:9 "(KJV) ⁹ And saith unto him, All these things will I give thee, if thou wilt fall down and worship me."** He will offer you the desires of one's heart through the lust of the eye, lust of the flesh, and the prides of this life.

His kingdom is now earthly and ruled through the hearts and minds of un-regenerated souls of men motivated by and through his seducing spirits. The diverse manifestation of these seducing spirits will show the inherent beastly nature of the fallen man that will cause him to embrace the nature of becoming subject to creatures he was given the authority to rule over to rule over.

There sole purpose is to reduce man to become servants of creatures and things in the Earth rather than his creator. We are born children of Satan; therefore, he will parade you before God as dehumanized degraded images of his creation, blinded and left with a servant mentality never knowing what spirit we are of until God brings us out of that darkness. Satan has been given the title deed to the Earth by Adam. **Matthew 4:7 "(KJV) ⁸ Again, the devil taketh him up into an exceeding high mountain, and sheweth him all the kingdoms of the world, and the glory of them;"** Jesus did not dispute with the devil about these earthly kingdoms because he knew how he got them. Now in God's image, man will serve the gods of this world by not knowing what spirit possesses him. The world and all its goods; without God, he has no way to resist these temptations. Through seminary seduction, he will show Christian leaders how to build their earthly kingdom in the name of God.

Man; The Brute Beast

This will become the nature of his fallen state as a brut beast; remember, Satan will have all creation available to his seducing spirits. We get a picture of this in his encounter with the Gergesenes man…**Matthew 8:28-32 "(KJV) ²⁸ And when he was come to the other side into the country of the Gergesenes, there met him two possessed with devils, coming out of the tombs, exceeding fierce, so that no man might pass by that way. ²⁹ And, behold, they cried out, saying, what have we to do with thee, Jesus, thou Son of God? art thou come hither to torment us before the time? ³⁰ And there was a good way off from them an herd of many swine feeding. ³¹ So the devils besought him, saying, If thou cast us out, suffer us to go away into the herd of swine. ³² And**

he said unto them. And when they were come out, they went into the herd of swine: and, behold, the whole herd of swine ran violently down a steep place into the sea, and perished in the waters". These spirits had a right to be in the world and manifest themselves in any living creature, such as the swines. However, these manifested as legions in that man were the type that create multiple personalities that can be destructive to your flesh. It is not uncommon to be possessed with more than one personality as human beings. That's the transfer in generational curses.

These spirits in animals of lesser degree than humans will change the nature of the beast it occupies and without you knowing, begin to control you, change your loyalties, and transform your mindset to their priorities. These are the spirits that create these organizations to protect themselves from humans by establishing animal rights organizations. This mindset is devoid of humans as being superior to them because these spirits will now rule over you. Human beings are the only species by nature, created in the image of God. In his condemned state, he walks up-right as a beast with superior intellect and abilities that will in-able him to lord over all creation in his evil state. He then, with-out knowing will be at war with other spirits in this realm with different natures than his own.

Because of his beastly nature, his flesh will become the means of his downfall. This is what will lead to him being rule by these lesser creatures such as those he willingly gave place that bounds him to a soul tie. This account for the loyalty people has to their pet animals that go beyond human reasoning and borders on becoming subject to your environment. These influences they have over you can change your priorities. I have been known to not take too kindly to spirits in animals having influences over my spirit as pets. They in my assessment of my life are hindrances because of the attention they require; like all things in this world, it is a matter of choice. We as fellow human beings allow ourselves to be controlled by things less than human as being created in the image of God. This is manifested without your knowledge of knowing you have subjected yourself to this degree. Many of us are not well treated by fellow human beings. This inherent weakness becomes the avenue of our vulnerabilities; therefore, these creatures can sense this and cause you to become attached to them. This is a form of a soul tie because they will feed on that weakness of longing for attention, these creatures will fill that void. **Ephesians 6:12 "KJV)** **¹² For we wrestle not against flesh and blood, but against principalities, against powers, against the <u>rulers of the darkness of this world,</u> against spiritual wickedness in high places."** Lack of knowledge of good and evil, caused us to be double minded in our action that will cause us to lack stability in our lives.

These have been some of my Solomon observations in this state of meditation in the spirit.

One part is ruled by Satan the other part is a subconscious knowledge of what is right but lack the will to do it such as what Paul explained in **Romans 7:15-25.** The rulers of darkness are manifested in flesh beings of God's creation, weather man or beast; the mystery of iniquity comes to us created in his image when Jesus reveals himself to you. Our entanglements in the cares and affairs of this life are the reasons for our shortcomings by our willing attachments to things that have no spiritual value in our relationship to the father. **Luke 8:14 "(KJV) 14 And that which fell among thorns are they, which, when they have heard, go forth, and are choked with cares and riches and pleasures of this life, and bring no fruit to perfection. Luke 21:34 (KJV) 34 And take heed to yourselves, lest at any time your hearts be overcharged with surfeiting, and drunkenness, and cares of this life, and so that day come upon you unawares. Galatians 5:1 (KJV) 1 Stand fast therefore in the liberty wherewith Christ hath made us free and be not entangled again with the yoke of bondage.** Anything that keeps you from performing the perfect will of God is considered a hinder or an entanglement.

Hebrews 5:12-13 "(KJV) 12 For when for the time ye ought to be teachers, ye have need that one teach you again which be the first principles of the oracles of God; and are become such as have need of milk, and not of strong meat. 1 Peter 3:18-20 (KJV) 18 For Christ also hath once suffered for sins, the just for the unjust, that he might bring us to God, being put to death in the flesh, but quickened by the Spirit: 19 By which also he went and preached unto the spirits in prison; 20 Which sometime were disobedient, when once the longsuffering of God waited in the days of Noah, while the ark was a preparing, wherein few, that is, eight souls were saved by water." Not to discern the times you're living can cause many of us who are caught in the cares and the affairs of this life to miss God's Day of visitation. All of God's creation of living things and human beings are potentials to become idols and gods through the deception of satanic seducing spirits. They can attach themselves to idols and living things. If our affections are not on things above, they are on things in the earth.

This is a constant temptation and warfare that trouble our minds daily of which without the power of the Holy Spirit, you will yield. That is the nature of our continuing in sin. **Matthew 24:13 (KJV) [13] But he that shall endure unto the end, the same shall be saved.**" There are not many that will endure the temptations of this world with out the love of Christ. **Hebrews 12:22 (KJV) [22] But ye are come unto mount Sion, and unto the city of the living God, the heavenly Jerusalem, and to an innumerable company of angels.**" This is the state of those whose mind is on heavenly things awaiting our redemption. After having been given these mysteries, it grieves me to know these things about the unseen world as to not know what we are dealing with. It is my love for God that keeps me with a sound mind through all this to the end. AMEN

Now on the national front

Historically, President trump's place in Biblical history is a mixture of Jehu & Cyrus of our times as a non-political leader, put in office by the Electoral College when there is a presidential election, too close to call by popular vote. His personal ego will make him a perfect candidate for our enemies to manipulate; particularly, the three Communist sisters, Russia, China and North Korea. He shows signs of being possessed with a dictator spirit; therefore, look for him to be more favorable to foreign dictators by his actions.

The Electoral College is the Republic's designee in each state to oversee that the election is just when all the votes are counted, they come together to confirm the winner by voting accordingly. Down through the years it has evolved into a political organization that now vote alone party lines. Therefore, when there is an election too close to call, they now have become the means to ensure their party gets their man in office as now representing a Republican majority.

They put George W Bush (the son) in office this way and now Donald Trump under the same conditions. This is their way of circumventing or over-ruling a close popular vote in a national presidential election. I said that President Obama would be the last president elected by the popular vote; some of you thought it was a false prediction when Trump was elected. Hillary commanded the popular vote under these same conditions. I also said that I did not see her as a world leader in these last days. Her husband's presidency would be the end of their rise to power. She became the cymbal of the rise of the Jezebel spirit we have seen recently that is leading a movement we as men have brought upon ourselves as our sins of abuse have returned upon us. Obama's presidency was an answer to the slave's prayers of hope and change.

Everything done in secret is being brought to light as those in the public eye as idols in their positions are being exposed. All these crooked TV evangelists are going to be exposed as their boasted pride let the people see just what they have done to rob their supporters to live extravagant lifestyles in the name of religion. The principality we let overtake the church, took prayer out of the schools. Now this last generation will become the killing grounds as these suicide demons are released upon them to fulfill a curse on this last generation. God is going to bring many of them to salvation as his mercy on them as innocent children for our hypocrisy that led them to this slaughter. They, as the last generation, were claimed with a cursed on them for our hypocrisy as a Christian nation. The sign upon them is revealed in the chronicle of **"Observations"**. Many are reserved to take their parents place in the coming great revival during the tribulation period. When God gave me this scripture in … **Isaiah 5:14 (KJV)** ¹⁴ **<u>Therefore hell hath enlarged herself and</u> opened her mouth without measure: and their glory, and <u>their multitude, and their pomp,</u> and he that rejoiceth, <u>shall descend into it."</u>** These volcano eruptions are natural sign, will also happen in more places. It will continue to run to the point of posing a threat to these Island.

Seducing spirits have used the media to reduce our attention span to moment by moment and hour by hour; therefore, most of you will forget this or reject it because you have been trained to only listen to men of renowned credibility you have put your trust with-out knowing that … **1 Corinthians 1:27 (KJV)** ²⁷ **But God hath chosen the foolish things of the world to confound the wise; and God hath chosen the weak things of the world to confound the things which are mighty; Philippians 3:3" (KJV)** ³ **For we are the circumcision, which worship God in the spirit, and rejoice in Christ Jesus, and have no confidence in the flesh."** We are to follow men as being examples in Christ as elects born from above. AMEN

The Wilderness Experience

God's instructions for those who are led into a Wilderness Experience, Consisting of You, God, and the Devil Just as Christ.

1. **Because of the perils of the times, your footsteps will be order by the lord. Psalm 37:23 (KJV) "23 The steps of a good man are ordered by the LORD: and he delighteth in his way. Isaiah 55:8 (KJV) ⁸ For my thoughts are not your thoughts, neither are your ways my ways, saith the LORD."** This is where you will be fully converted to save yourself

from the wrath to come in glory by making your calling and election sure. **2 Peter 1:10 (KJV) [10] Wherefore the rather, brethren, give diligence to make your calling and election sure: for if ye do these things, ye shall never fall:**

2. Every one that endures the wilderness will know Christ for them self. **Isaiah 53:1 (KJV) "1 Who hath believed our report? and to whom is the arm of the LORD revealed? Daniel 11:22 (KJV) [22] And with the arms of a flood shall they be overflown from before him, and shall be broken; yea, also the prince of the covenant. Romans 8:27 (KJV) [27] And he that searcheth the hearts knoweth what is the mind of the Spirit, because he maketh intercession for the saints according to the will of God."**

3. All who entertain fear, doubt and unbelief will get you destroyed in the wilderness and you shall not see God as in the days if Moses. **Matthew 10:28 (KJV) "28 And fear not them which kill the body, but are not able to kill the soul: but rather fear him which is able to destroy both soul and body in hell. 2 Thessalonians 2:10 (KJV) [10] And with all deceivableness of unrighteousness in them that perish; because they received not the love of the truth, that they might be saved."**

4. All who will endure the wilderness will have the same spirit and will know one another. **1 John 4:6 (KJV) "6 We are of God: he that knoweth God heareth us; he that is not of God heareth not us. Hereby know we the spirit of truth, and the spirit of error. 1 John 2:20 (KJV) [20] But ye have an unction from the Holy One, and ye know all things."**

5. You will be led through fasting, prayer and the study of the word. **2 Timothy 2:15 (KJV) "15 Study to shew thyself approved unto God, a workman that needeth not to be ashamed, rightly dividing the word of truth. Zechariah 7:5 (KJV) [5] Speak unto all the people of the land, and to the priests, saying, when ye fasted and mourned in the fifth and seventh month, even those seventy years, did ye at all fast unto me, even to me?** Before the natural temple was destroyed, none of his people sought him for a vision of time of his return. Only my chosen elected apostles were given this vision.

Satan's Role While You are in the Wilderness.

1. Satan will try to deceive you to go down the broad road. **Matthew 7:14-15 (KJV) ¹⁴ Because strait is the gate, and narrow is the way, which leadeth unto life, and few there be that find it.** He will contend with you to keep you from separating from all the Holy Spirit is leading you to do. **¹⁵ Beware of false prophets, which come to you in sheep's clothing, but inwardly they are ravening wolves. Isaiah 50:7 (KJV) ⁷ For the Lord GOD will help me; therefore, shall I not be confounded: therefore have I set my face like a flint, and I know that I shall not be ashamed."**

2. Satan will show you all you are giving up that is yours but his way. **Matthew 4:9 (KJV) "9 And saith unto him, All these things will I give thee, if thou wilt fall down and worship me."** Your knowledge of the word will be tested. **Matthew 4:4 (KJV) ⁴ But he answered and said, It is written, Man shall not live by bread alone, but by every word that proceedeth out of the mouth of God. Matthew 4:10 (KJV) ¹⁰ Then saith Jesus unto him, get thee hence, Satan: for it is written, Thou shalt worship the Lord thy God, and him only shalt thou serve.**

3. When you are led into the wilderness, don't' be anxious but try every spirit whether it be of God. **2 Chronicles 34:27 (KJV) ²⁷ Because thine heart was tender, and thou didst humble thyself before God, when thou heardest his words against this place, and against the inhabitants thereof, and humbledst thyself before me, and didst rend thy clothes, and weep before me; I have even heard thee also, saith the LORD. Romans 12:1-2 (NLT) ¹ And so, dear brothers and sisters, I plead with you to give your bodies to God. Let them be a living and holy sacrifice—the kind he will accept. When you think of what he has done for you, is this too much to ask? ² Don't copy the behavior and customs of this world, but let God transform you into a new person by changing the way you think. Then you will know what God wants you to do, and you will know how good and pleasing and perfect his will really is."**

4. God will let Satan try you for a season as to purify you as his temple. **1 Peter 4:12 (KJV) " ¹² Beloved, think it not strange concerning the fiery trial which is to try you, as though some strange thing happened unto you: 1 Peter 5:10 (KJV) ¹⁰ But the God of all grace, who hath called us unto his eternal glory by Christ Jesus, after that ye have suffered a while, make you perfect, stablish, strengthen, settle you."** All end time saints chosen by election are in waiting to

become the John the Baptist to carry the message to revive this apostate church world.

5. Those that endure the wilderness experience will walk in the fullness of the "Kingly, Priestly and the Prophetic anointing of Christ. **Hebrews 1:9 (KJV) "9 Thou hast loved righteousness, and hated iniquity; therefore God, even thy God, hath anointed thee with the oil of gladness above thy fellows. 2 Corinthians 1:21 (KJV) [21] Now he which stablisheth us with you in Christ, and hath anointed us, is God;"**

What will be the difference the world will see in all those who endure their wilderness experience?

1. Your appearance will be like as unto Moses when you come out in the fullness. **2 Corinthians 5:17 (KJV) " [17] Therefore if any man be in Christ, he is a new creature: old things are passed away; behold, all things are become new."**

2. You will represent the fullness of the God head bodily which we have never achieved to this day. This is why … **Mark 13:20 (KJV) "20 And except that the Lord had shortened those days, no flesh should be saved: but for the elect's sake, whom he hath chosen, he hath shortened the days."** Whether you believe it are not … **Isaiah 53:5-6 (KJV) " [5] But he was wounded for our transgressions, he was bruised for our iniquities: the chastisement of our peace was upon him; and with his stripes we are healed. [6] All we like sheep have gone astray; we have turned everyone to his own way; and the LORD hath laid on him the iniquity of us all."** In time past, our wilderness experience was cut short by the teachings and the traditions of mans theological interpretations of the gospel that has led us down this road to the state of an apostate church.

3. We will be prepared to make war with the principalities and powers of darkness as in … **Ephesians 6:1(KJV) [12] For we wrestle not against flesh and blood, but against principalities, against powers, against the rulers of the darkness of this world, against spiritual wickedness in high places. Ephesians 4:12 (KJV) [12] for the perfecting of the saints, for the work of the ministry, for the edifying of the body of Christ:**

4. He will begin to judge the world through your vessel. **1 Corinthians 6:2- (KJV)" 2 Do ye not know that the saints shall judge the world? and if the world shall be judged by you, are ye unworthy to judge the smallest matters? 3 Know ye not that we shall judge angels? how much more things that pertain to this life?** (In time of tribulation … **Proverbs 29:16 (KJV)16 When the wicked are multiplied, transgression increaseth: but the righteous shall see their fall. 2 Tim. 3:13 (KJV) 13 But evil men and seducers shall wax worse and worse, deceiving, and being deceived.**

5. The whole world will see the perfect man in this generation … **Matthew 5:48 (KJV) "48 Be ye therefore perfect, even as your Father which is in heaven is perfect."**

6. The fear of God will return to the assembly. **Psalm 66:16 (KJV) " 16 Come and hear, all ye that fear God, and I will declare what he hath done   for my soul. Ecclesiastes 12:13 (KJV) 13 Let us hear the conclusion of the whole matter: Fear God and keep his commandments: for this is the whole duty of man."** The return of the gospel of Jesus Christ will once again arrest the attention of the world and present to the world the only God.

A call to perfect love

Matthew 22:36-39 (KJV) "36 Master, which is the great commandment in the law? 37 Jesus said unto him, thou shalt love the Lord thy God with all thy heart, and with all thy soul, and with all thy mind. 38 This is the first and great commandment. 39 And the second is like unto it, thou shalt love thy neighbour as thyself. 1 John 4:18 (KJV) 18 There is no fear in love; but perfect love casteth out fear: because fear hath torment. He that feareth is not made perfect in love." Our separation into the wilderness is a repeat of the same wilderness as his people in these last days as a type and shadow of Christ entering into the wilderness in you to be crucified to death and become meat for the master's use. **2 Corinthians 6:17 (KJV) "17 Wherefore come out from among them, and be ye separate, saith the Lord, and touch not the unclean thing; and I will receive you, Matthew 4:1 (KJV) 1 Then was Jesus led up of the Spirit into the wilderness to be tempted of the devil."**

We are going through many changes as being tested to be brought into perfection. Those that endure this wilderness will walk in the fullness of Christ as he did when he came out of his wilderness. This time he will walk you through this wilderness in your temple to do the greater works. **John 14:30 (KJV "30 Hereafter I will not talk much with you: for the prince of this world cometh, and hath nothing in me. Luke 4:14 (KJV) ¹⁴ And Jesus returned in the power of the Spirit into Galilee: and there went out a fame of him through all the region round about."**

The world will once again see what this present apostasy has failed to produce. Ninety-eight percent of the church world is not in a place spiritually to heed to the call to repent from these prophets and messengers.

Our affections are being set on heaven and going home. **Colossians 3:2 (KJV) "2 Set your affection on things above, not on things on the earth. Luke 21:34 (KJV) ³⁴ And take heed to yourselves, lest at any time your hearts be overcharged with surfeiting, and drunkenness, and cares of this life, and so that day come upon you unawares. James 1:12 (KJV) ¹² Blessed is the man that endureth temptation: for when he is tried, he shall receive the crown of life, which the Lord hath promised to them that love him.** You will not be led into this wilderness until you fully surrender to the leading of the Holy Spirit. This is to those that live in the reality of being born again. **John 16:13 (KJV) ¹³ Howbeit when he, the Spirit of truth, is come, he will guide you into all truth: for he shall not speak of himself; but whatsoever he shall hear, that shall he speak: and he will shew you things to come. 1 John 4:9 (KJV) ⁹ In this was manifested the love of God toward us, because that God sent his only begotten Son into the world, that we might live through him. Matthew 10:16 (KJV) ¹⁶ Behold, I send you forth as sheep in the midst of wolves: be ye therefore wise as serpents, and harmless as doves.** You are being prepared as vessels for this last day move in glory beyond your comprehension. You will posses the fullness of the mind of Christ. **1 "Cor. 2:16 ¹⁶ For who hath known the mind of the Lord, that he may instruct him? But we have the mind of Christ."** This wilderness will bring the death of your flesh. **1 Corinthians 7:29 (KJV) ²⁹ But this I say, brethren, the time is short: it remaineth, that both they that have wives be as though they had none; 2 Corinthians 5:17 (KJV) ¹⁷ Therefore if any man be in Christ, he is a new creature: old things are passed away; behold, all things are become new.** All will suffer to bring glory to his body. **1 Peter 4:1 (KJV) " ¹ Forasmuch then as Christ hath suffered for us in the flesh, arm yourselves likewise with the same mind: for he that hath suffered in the flesh hath ceased from sin;"** All who are called will walk in the unity of the faith. **Ephesians 4:13 (KJV) "13 Till we all come in the unity of the faith, and of the knowledge of the Son of God, unto a perfect man, unto the measure of the stature of the fulness of Christ:"** All will rest from their labor. **Hebrews 4:9 (KJV) " ⁹ There remaineth therefore a rest to the**

people of God. Colossians 2:9 (KJV) ⁹ For in him dwelleth all the fulness of the Godhead bodily." This is the rest that allows Christ to have complete control of the vessel. **1 Thessalonians 5:23 (KJV) ²³ And the very God of peace sanctify you wholly; and I pray God your whole spirit and soul and body be preserved blameless unto the coming of our Lord Jesus Christ.**

This is God's warning to those who have heard this revelation that will cause you to be cut off.

1. God is walking in the earth selecting his people to be used; he will not tolerate disobedience.

2. Keep your eyes on God and not on the circumstances.

3. Remember Akin and Eli's judgment that cause their whole household to be lost because of their disobedience.

4. We are called to a total sacrifice of our will. Except you are willing to forsake all, you will not lead his people.

5. Let your words be few and seasoned with grace. Avoid idol chatter and worldly conversations that leads babblings and judging.

6. You must learn to resist Satan's seducing spirits that will try to deceive you.

7. You will face many trials and circumstances that will try to prevent you from coming out the wilderness. These trials are to purify you.

8. All these trials are design to bring you into full submission to perform his will.

9. When you have fully surrender, don't look back to those things you left behind. Remember lot's wife.

10. Cast all your cares upon him completely and put him first.

11. Waite for his instructions in ever thing by prayer.

12. Live in a conscious state that you are not your own.

13. All your sacrifices are not that important to God; only you obedience.

14. Subject yourselves to one another and your leaders.

15. When you feel a burden, seek the lord for the answer before you move.

16. Always be sensitive to the spirit.

Romans 14:13 (KJV) [13] Let us not therefore judge one another anymore: but judge this rather, that no man put a stumbling block or an occasion to fall in his brother's way. 2 Corinthians 13:11 (KJV) [11] Finally, brethren, farewell. Be perfect, be of good comfort, be of one mind, live in peace; and the God of love and peace shall be with you. In my personal testimony, my first wilderness experience brought me to Phoenix, Az. This has been my training ground all these years to perfect my fruit. Those experiences cause me the lost of all things to find God. The lord revealed to me that my life's parallels will be similar to that of Moses. When all is completed, I will have gone through two wilderness experiences and the lost of all things again to keep him. The first was to prepare me for the second as a deliverer of his people. The above revelations and instruction are for those elected to enter into the wilderness experience.

All these instructions are for the elects given with ears to hear what the spirit is saying to his elects of the last day move of God that will arrest the attention of the world.

Observations of a Messenger

Those of you who have a copy of my latest book entitled **"Biblical Prophetical Chronicles of the Last Generation,"** Subtitled: **Revelation; the Final Layer Revealed"** containing the third layer of the book of Revelation; these are some added insights of later revelations. Some have said, this was a hard read; but convincing truth not taught to this degree in the churches. It has been my greatest revelations out of this experience to hear the **"Great I Am"** speak to me in a clear voice through the Holy Spirit to write these revelations down. Since we are the lease known, this word will be for those who have been given ears to hear.

Romans 1:13 "(KJV) ¹³ Now I would not have you ignorant, brethren, that oftentimes I purposed to come unto you, (but was let hitherto,) that I might have some fruit among you also, even as among other Gentiles." When you read under the anointing of the Holy Spirit, he shows you the deeper layered revelations with-in the verses of scriptures. Since God uses whom he will speak through, Paul in the above verse speak with a deeper interpretive meaning as follows. When you live in the reality of God in you, you will not be ignorant of the right context meaning of the word for your times. This is that deeper layer … **"The Holy Spirit desired to have full possession of you when he arrived; however, your thought and ways hindered him from demonstrating the full capabilities of your newfound potential as to walk in the fullness of faith; therefore, he could not fully represent the father as he did in Christ."** Now that's our shortcomings by our sins of omission as being entangled in the cares of this life will lack the full knowledge revelation.

Many are lead to go down the broad road of destruction; through false teachings from well-meaning pastors and teachers. That's the road who's fruits are identified in **Gal. 5:19-21**. These are your luke-warm confessing Christians, living in spiritual compromised conditions that bring no glory to God but to flesh as men seek to have the glory of men and themselves. They are not on sound biblical standards of true holiness. When the Holy Spirit is in charge of the assembly, the people are taught by God himself. This is Jesus returned in the spirit that confirms his presents … people are healed, delivered, and set free from demon spirits. I am very skeptical as not keeping company with people I'm not led to be with that doesn't have ears to hear the real truth as it's demonstrated in the power of true holiness. That's because, I want to see these miracles done through me when I come out of this wilderness.

Not that I'm a judge, I just don't want the devil to justify destroying my flesh for lack of knowledge for keeping company with spiritual leaders that won't declare the whole council of the truth. **Ephesians 5:11 "(KJV) ¹¹ And have no fellowship with the unfruitful works of darkness, but rather reprove them. Amos 3:3 (KJV) ³ Can two walk together, except they be agreed?"** The fruit of many of these organized religions is genetically altered with strands of Satan's DNA. What I have observed in these new doctrines of rapture and prosperity, too many are making provisions for the flesh in a show of Godliness as to gain material possessions only. There is no mention of self-denial and seeking the welfare of others. **1 Corinthians 15:31 "(KJV) ³¹ I protest by your rejoicing which I have in Christ Jesus our Lord, I die daily."** Now if Paul and Jesus is our example as to the right path as now having our minds on heavenly things, then we should have this mind-set … **Colossians 3:1 (KJV) ¹ If ye then be risen with Christ, seek those things which are above, where Christ sitteth on the right hand of God.** We who are born from above have the mind of Christ as … **1 Corinthians 2:2 "(KJV) ² For I determined not to know anything among you, save Jesus Christ, and him crucified."** Jesus strive to never comment about the obvious among people born in sin; they can't help what they do under the influence of the devil. That's why He went about doing good.

He was looking beyond their obvious sins to show them what they needed. When God told me what kind of faith he seeks to find in every believer, which should be our goal, I knew then that he was asking me not to doubt his word but stand on it to see him perform it. **Jeremiah 1:12 "(KJV) ¹² Then said the LORD unto me, Thou hast well seen: for I will hasten my word to perform it."** I readily saw that what he was requiring of me, meant total surrender in spirit, soul, and body. God is not into earthly kingdom building; that's why he said … **Colossians 3:2 "(KJV) ² Set your affection on things above, not on things on the earth."** The persecution and rejection that the early Christians faced was for not compromising this truth unto death. **2 Timothy 3:12 "(KJV) ¹² Yea, and all that will live godly in Christ Jesus shall suffer persecution."** Therefore, if I believe he **is,** then everything that is happening to me is him taking the abuse in my body knowing that I already have the victory. Now that's the faith he seeks to find.

The thought that boarders on pride is to think we are something; in God's sight, we are but a mass of dirt mold in his image, breathing his breath and living in the life he gave you. That's all he has asked for is that body with his spirit and life to put his intellect (knowledge) in that gives you his soul and all we have to do to live for eternity is to just do what ever he has told you to do and be faithful until your time of your departure.

Doing good is a matter of conscious convictions as a sinner until you are provoked, then, the degree of restraint as to what you will do will show at that time. That's why we have to be tested so we can see the need of God's power in our newfound ability not to yield. During the learning process of time … **Romans 8:28 "(KJV) ²⁸ And we know that all things work together for good to them that love God, to them who are the called according to his purpose."** This is what I have found out by observation from truth; Don't be surprised when you take this stand, you may find yourself among the few. His called-out ones as his elects, born from above have been preserved for his use before the foundation of the world for a time such as this. He has set all things in motions as knowing the end from the beginning. **Isaiah 46:10 "(KJV) ¹⁰ Declaring the end from the beginning, and from ancient times the things that are not yet done, saying, my counsel shall stand, and I will do all my pleasure:"** My beloved brothers and sisters, you won't know what deliverance is until you can be transparent to the point of humble humility where there's no pride left in you. I have also observed that the worst of sinners make the best Christians. They will only follow those that stand in truth without compromise. They, in many cases were condemned while in the world.

We are all going to die. **Hebrews 9:27 "(KJV) ²⁷ And as it is appointed unto men once to die, but after this the judgment:"** Whether you are a believer or not, you are going to meet him that gave you this life in the judgment. You will be rewarded for how you chose to live it in this short span here on earth. So, for the benefit of those who get to read these chronicles as a skeptic, none will escape these realities. Having been given this revelation, I have no choice but to die from self so He can get the glory out of this body of death. **Luke 12:48 "(KJV) ⁴⁸ But he that knew not, and did commit things worthy of stripes, shall be beaten with few stripes. For unto whomsoever much is given, of him shall be much required: and to whom men have committed much, of him they will ask the more."1 Thessalonians 4:7 "(KJV) ⁷ For God hath not called us unto uncleanness, but unto holiness."** AMEN

Now on the National Front

I was asked about what I see in this last generation that seem to be caught up in an epidemic of body art; such as tattoo and piercings all over their entire body in conventions for the sole purpose of exposing their body art and piercings. God's forbids his people from marking their bodies in this manner … **Leviticus 19:28-29 "(KJV) ²⁸ Ye shall not make any cuttings in your flesh for the dead,** (These type spirits will mark you according to your extent of evil skeletal heads of the dead.) **nor print any marks upon you:** (The type of tattoo can be a claim mark on your flesh in the spirit world.) **I am the LORD. ²⁹ Do not prostitute thy daughter,** (God foreknew that Satan put a curse on this last generation that can only come to pass if we break our national covenant as a nation.) **to cause her to be a whore;** (The curse of sodomy on our land will give him the right to take our young daughters as payment for all the aborted babies.) **lest the land fall to whoredom, and the land become full of wickedness."**

I recall being in a meeting in 1998, hearing a prayer walking prophet whom God sent all over the world to break cures on lands. I recall him saying, he was walking on a Native American reservation that had descended from an Mexican Aztec Indian tribe. As soon as he put foot on that land, he fell very ill and inquired to the lord as to the reason he could not speak over that tribal land? He was told that they were a powerful war tribe that was wiped out during the resettlement of America. They put a curse over this nation on the last generation.

This was their appearance; they had tattoos all over their bodies and piercing on their body parts. They beat loud drums that can be heard all around the area. This curse would come in the form of a sign that would indicate the last generation where-in their spirit would return in them. I was quickened in my spirit when I began to see and increase in a spirit that was causing this epidemic of tattoos and body art with piercings in all parts of their bodies. I noticed it started in the poor neighborhoods with loud boom box music. This was in 2010 when loud derogatory rap was accompanied with loud base music that caught my attention. I noticed from that time to 2017 over a period of seven years, over 60% percent of the American population have some form of a tattoo along with piercings on their body parts. I inquired about the validity of this sign? The curse could only be manifested if we as a nation departed from our Christian roots. The fall of the church into divisions is how these spirits gained the momentum we see today that has produced this sign.

2 Thessalonians 2:3 "(KJV) ³ Let no man deceive you by any means: for that day shall not come, except there come a falling away first, and that man of sin be revealed, the son of perdition;" Now the evidence of this sign being fulfilled, coupled with the spirit Sodomy being released. Now on our beaches and in public gatherings, you see this being demonstrated when they take off their clothes and parade in their colored under-ware to show off their body art. An epidemic of abductions unreported of young girls are being sold in the underground sex trade. These are the same demons that pimp these young girls with-out any regard to their humanity. This is the return of the same spirit during the slave trade era that brought people of color to this nation and treated them in a none humans, taking these young Anglos, Asian and Hispanic girls to sale as putting in orders for livestock.

Look around at your daughters and grand-daughters how they are scantily dressed that make them easy targets for these men possessed with these demons. What we have not been taught about the spirit world is where we see them taking the lives of the young school children which has become the killing grounds for these suicide demons now released form the pit. They are mass-murdering demons in legions to possess those given over to Satan for destruction.

When they have completed their task, they then cause the host to be killed. The vast majority of this generation have been raised with -out a sense of reality or responsibility; therefore, they are raised up as an accident waiting to happen. The mercy of God is upon many of them that will take the place of their luke-warm parents that delivered them into the hands of these cold-hearted merciless demon possessed mediums rising in this generation that sacrificed their children to the devil for the prides of this life.

They are suffering this curse upon them for our hypocrisy. These final updated chronicles are the completed revelations to this generation. I know these are some hard words and many have departed my company as they did most of the apostles for speaking truth. **2 Timothy 3:12 (KJV) ¹² Yea, and all that will live godly in Christ Jesus shall suffer persecution. John 15:18 (KJV) ¹⁸ If the world hate you, ye know that it hated me before it hated you.**

May God have mercy on all that repent and turn from our wicked ways. AMEN.

Your End Time Messenger

Steven B Riddley